New Perspectives on
Microsoft®
PowerPoint 7
for Windows® 95

BRIEF

Beverly B. Zimmerman
Brigham Young University

S. Scott Zimmerman
Brigham Young University

A Susan Solomon Book

COURSE

COURSE TECHNOLOGY, INC.
A DIVISION OF COURSE TECHNOLOGY
COMMUNICATIONS GROUP
ONE MAIN STREET, CAMBRIDGE MA 02142
AN INTERNATIONAL THOMSON PUBLISHING COMPANY

I(T)P

Albany • Bonn • Boston • Cincinnati • London • Madrid • Melbourne • Mexico City
New York • Paris • San Francisco • Singapore • Tokyo • Toronto • Washington

New Perspectives on Microsoft PowerPoint 7 for Windows 95 — Brief is published by Course Technology, Inc.

Managing Editor	Mac Mendelsohn
Series Consulting Editor	Susan Solomon
Senior Product Manager	Barbara Clemens
Production Editor	Christine Spillett
Text and Cover Designer	Ella Hanna
Cover Illustrator	Nancy Nash

© 1996 by Course Technology, Inc.
A Division of International Thomson Publishing, Inc.

For more information contact:

Course Technology, Inc.
One Main Street
Cambridge, MA 02142

International Thomson Editores
Campos Eliseos 385, Piso 7
Col. Polanco
11560 Mexico D.F. Mexico

International Thomson Publishing Europe
Berkshire House 168-173
High Holborn
London WCIV 7AA
England

International Thomson Publishing GmbH
Königswinterer Strasse 418
53227 Bonn
Germany

Thomas Nelson Australia
102 Dodds Street
South Melbourne, 3205
Victoria, Australia

International Thomson Publishing Asia
211 Henderson Road
#05-10 Henderson Building
Singapore 0315

Nelson Canada
1120 Birchmount Road
Scarborough, Ontario
Canada M1K 5G4

International Thomson Publishing Japan
Hirakawacho Kyowa Building, 3F
2-2-1 Hirakawacho
Chiyoda-ku, Tokyo 102
Japan

Trademarks

Course Technology and the open book logo are registered trademarks of Course Technology, Inc.

I(T)P The ITP logo is a trademark under license.

Microsoft PowerPoint and Windows 95 are registered trademarks of Microsoft Corporation.

Some of the product names and company names used in this book have been used for identification purposes only and may be trademarks or registered trademarks of their respective manufacturers and sellers.

Disclaimer

Course Technology, Inc. reserves the right to revise this publication and make changes from time to time in its content without notice.

ISBN 0-7600-3547-4

Printed in the United States of America

10 9 8 7 6 5 4 3 2 1

Preface The New Perspectives Series

What is the New Perspectives Series?

Course Technology, Inc.'s **New Perspectives Series** combines text and technology products that teach computer concepts and microcomputer applications. Users consistently praise this series for its innovative pedagogy, creativity, supportive and engaging style, accuracy, and its use of interactive technology. The first **New Perspectives** text was published in January of 1993. Since then, the series has grown to more than thirty titles and has become the best-selling series on computer concepts and microcomputer applications. Others have imitated the New Perspectives features, design, and technology, but none have replicated its quality and its ability to consistently meet and anticipate the needs of instructors and students.

New Perspectives microcomputer applications books are available in seven categories—Brief, Introductory, Intermediate, Comprehensive, Advanced, Four-in-One, and Five-in-One.

Brief books are about 100 pages long and are intended to teach only the essentials about the particular microcomputer application. The book you are holding is a Brief book.

Introductory books are about 300 pages and consist of 6 or 7 tutorials. An Introductory book is designed for a short course on a particular application or for a one-term course to be used in combination with other introductory books. **Four-in-One** books and **Five-in-One** books combine a Brief book on Windows with 3 or 4 Introductory books.

Comprehensive books consist of all of the tutorials in the Introductory book, plus 3 or 4 more tutorials on more advanced topics. They also include the Brief Windows tutorials, Additional Cases, and a Reference Section.

Intermediate books take the 3 or 4 tutorials at the end of three Comprehensive books and combine them. The Additional Cases and Reference Sections are also included.

Advanced books cover topics similar to those in the Comprehensive tutorials, but in more depth. Advanced books present the most high-level coverage in the series.

Finally, as the name suggests, **Concepts and Applications** books combine our *New Perspectives on Computer Concepts* book with various brief and introductory microcomputer applications books.

New
Perspectives
Series
Applications
Titles

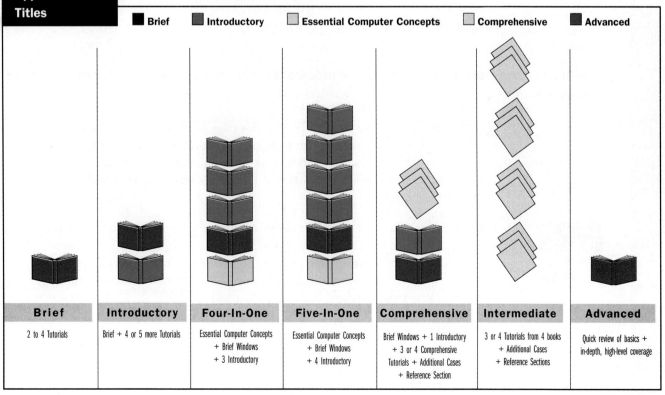

Brief	Introductory	Four-In-One	Five-In-One	Comprehensive	Intermediate	Advanced
2 to 4 Tutorials	Brief + 4 or 5 more Tutorials	Essential Computer Concepts + Brief Windows + 3 Introductory	Essential Computer Concepts + Brief Windows + 4 Introductory	Brief Windows + 1 Introductory + 3 or 4 Comprehensive Tutorials + Additional Cases + Reference Section	3 or 4 Tutorials from 4 books + Additional Cases + Reference Sections	Quick review of basics + in-depth, high-level coverage

Legend: ■ Brief ■ Introductory □ Essential Computer Concepts □ Comprehensive ■ Advanced

How do the Windows 95 editions differ from the Windows 3.1 editions?

Aside from the obvious change—covering Windows 95 software instead of 3.1 software—we've made several changes in the Windows 95 editions of the **New Perspectives Series**. We listened to instructors who use the series and made the changes they've asked us to make—to make this series even better.

Larger Page Size If you've used a **New Perspectives** text before, you'll immediately notice the book your holding is larger than our Windows 3.1 series books. We've responded to user requests for a larger page, which allows for larger screen shots and associated callouts.

Sessions We've divided the Tutorials into sessions. Each session is designed to be completed in about 45 minutes to an hour (depending, of course, upon special student needs and the speed of your lab equipment). With sessions, learning is broken up into more easily-assimilated "chunks." You can more accurately allocate time in your syllabus. Students can more easily manage the available lab time. Each session begins with a "session box," which quickly describes what skills the student will learn in the session. Furthermore, each session is numbered, making it easier for you and your students to navigate and communicate about the tutorial.

Quick Checks Each session concludes with meaningful, conceptual questions—called Quick Checks—that test students' understanding of what they learned in the session. The answers to all of the Quick Questions are at the back of the book, preceding the Index.

New Design We have retained a design that helps students easily differentiate between what they are to *do* and what they are to *read*. The steps are easily identified by their color background and numbered steps. Furthermore, this new design presents steps and screen shots in a larger, easier to read format.

What features are retained in the Windows 95 editions of the New Perspectives Series?

"Read This Before You Begin" Page This page is consistent with Course Technology's unequaled commitment to helping instructors introduce technology into the classroom. Technical considerations and assumptions about hardware and software are listed in one place to help instructors save time and eliminate unnecessary aggravation.

Tutorial Case Each tutorial begins with a problem presented in a case that is meaningful to students. The problem turns the task of learning how to use an application into a problem-solving process. The problems increase in complexity with each tutorial. These cases touch on multicultural, international, and ethical issues—so important to today's business curriculum.

1.
2.
3.

Step-by-Step Methodology The Course Technology step-by-step methodology keeps students on track. They click or press keys always within the context of solving the problem posed in the Tutorial Case. The text constantly guides students, letting them know where they are in the course of solving the problem. In addition, the numerous screen shots include labels that direct students' attention to what they should look at on the screen. On almost every page in this book, you can find an example of how steps, screen shots, and callouts work together.

TROUBLE?

TROUBLE? Paragraphs Trouble paragraphs anticipate the mistakes that students are likely to make and help them recover from these mistakes. By putting these paragraph in the book, rather than in the instructor's manual, we facilitate independent learning and free the instructor to focus on substantive conceptual issues rather than on common procedural errors.

Reference Windows Reference Windows appear throughout the text. This feature is specially designed and written so students can refer to them when doing the Tutorial Assignments and Case Problems, and after completing the course.

Task Reference The Task Reference is a summary of how to perform commonly-used tasks using the most efficient method, as well as helpful shortcuts.

Tutorial Assignments, Case Problems, and Lab Assignments Each tutorial concludes with Tutorial Assignments, which provide students additional hands-on practice of the skills they learned in the tutorial. The Tutorial Assignments are followed by four Case Problems that have approximately the same scope as the Tutorial Case. In Windows 95 applications texts, there are always one Case Problems in the book and one in the Instructor's Manual that do not use a presupplied student file, requiring students to solve problems from scratch. Finally, if a Lab (see below) accompanies the tutorial, Lab Assignments are included.

Exploration Exercises The Windows environment allows students to learn by exploring and discovering what they can do. Exploration Exercises can be Tutorial Assignments or Case Problems that encourage students to explore the capabilities of the program they are using and to extend their knowledge using the Windows Help facility and other reference materials.

The New Perspectives Series is known for using technology to help instructors teach and administer, and to help students learn. What technology components are available with this textbook? What are Course Tools?

All the teaching and learning materials available with the **New Perspectives Series** are known as Course Tools.

Course Test Manager Course Test Manager is a cutting edge Windows-based testing software that helps instructors design and administer pre-tests, practice tests, and actual examinations. The full-featured program provides random test generation of practice tests, immediate on-line feedback, and generation of detailed study guides for questions that are incorrectly answered. On-line pre-tests help instructors assess student skills and plan instruction. Also, students can take tests at the computer, which can be automatically graded and generate statistical information for the instructor on student individual and group performance. Instructors can also use Course Test Manager to produce printed tests.

Course Presenter Course Presenter is a CD ROM-based presentation tool that provides instructors a wealth of resources for use in the classroom, replacing traditional overhead transparencies with computer-generated screenshows. Presenter gives instructors the flexibility to create custom presentations, complete with matching students notes and lecture notes pages. The presentations are closely coordinated with the content of the New Perspectives book and other Course Tools, and provide another resource to help instructors to teach the way they want to teach.

Online Companion When you use a **New Perspectives** product, you are able to access Course Technology's Online Companion. Instructors may enter the Faculty Online Companion for additional instructors' materials. Please see your Instructor's Manual or call your Course Technology customer service representative for more information. Students may access their Online Companion in the Student Center on the World Wide Web at http://www.vmedia.com/cti/.

Instructor's Manual **New Perspectives** Instructor's Manuals are written by the author(s) and are quality assurance tested. Each Instructor's Manual includes some or all of the following items:

- Answers and solutions to all of the Quick Checks, Tutorial Assignments, Case Problems, and Additional Cases. Suggested solutions are also included for the Exploration Exercises. This is available in hard copy and digital form.
- A Student Files disk containing all of the data files that students will use for the Tutorials, Tutorial Assignments, and Case Problems.
- Troubleshooting Tips, which anticipate commonly-encountered problems.
- Extra Problems and Additional Cases, to augment teaching options.
- Instructor's Notes, prepared by the authors and based on their teaching experience.

Acknowledgments

The authors would like to thank the following reviewers for their valuable feedback on this very exciting project: Sherri Cady, Anoka-Ramsey Community College; Emily Ketcham, Baylor University; Catherine Rathke, College of DuPage, and Linda Wise Miller, University of Idaho.

Also special thanks to: Susan Solomon, Series Consulting Editor; Mac Mendelsohn, Managing Editor; Barbara Clemens, Product Manager; Christine Spillett, Production Editor; Jim Valente, Quality Assurance Supervisor, and student testers Chris Hall, Christopher Lathrop, and Tia McCarthy.

Finally, we would like to thank Jessica Evans, our developmental editor, for her cheerful encouragement, expert assistance, and friendly support.

Beverly B. Zimmerman
S. Scott Zimmerman

Table of **Contents**

TUTORIAL 4

Presenting a Slide Show

Annual Report of Inca Imports International

New Perspectives on

Microsoft® PowerPoint 7
for Windows® 95

BRIEF

TUTORIALS

Read This **Before You Begin**

STUDENT DISKS

To complete the tutorials, Tutorial Assignments, and Cases in this book, you need six Student Disks. Your instructor will either provide you with Student Disks or ask you to make your own.

If you are supposed to make your own Student Disks, you will need six blank, formatted disks. You will need to copy a set of folders from a file server or standalone computer onto your disks. Your instructor will tell you which computer, drive letter, and folders contain the folders you need. The following table shows you which folders go on each of your disks, so that you will have enough disk space to complete all the tutorials, Tutorial Assignments, and Cases:

Disk	Write this on the disk label	Put these folders on the disk
1	Student Disk 1: Tutorial 1	Tutorial.01
2	Student Disk 2: Tutorial 2	Tutorial.02
3	Student Disk 3: Tutorial 3 and Tutorial Assignments	Tutorial.03
4	Student Disk 4: Tutorial 3 Cases	Tutorial.03
5	Student Disk 5: Tutorial 4	Tutorial.04
6	Pack and Go Wizard: Tutorial 4	Format disk and leave blank

When you begin each tutorial, be sure you are using the correct Student Disk. See the inside front or inside back cover of this book for more information on Student Disks, or ask your instructor or technical support person for assistance.

USING YOUR OWN COMPUTER

If you are going to work through this book using your own computer, you need:

■ **Computer system** Microsoft Windows 95 and Microsoft PowerPoint 7 for Windows 95 must be installed on your computer. This book assumes a Standard installation of PowerPoint.

■ **The Student Disks** Ask your instructor or lab manager for details on how to get the Student Disks. You will not be able to complete the tutorials or exercises in this book using your own computer until you have Student Disks.

VISIT OUR WORLD WIDE WEB SITE

Additional materials designed especially for you are available on the World Wide Web. Go to http://www.vmedia.com/cti/.

To complete the tutorials in this book, your students must use a set of Student Files. These files are stored on the Student Files Disk that is included with the Instructor's Manual. Follow the instructions on the disk label and the Readme.doc file to uncompress and copy them to your server or standalone computer. You can view the Readme.doc file using WordPad.

Once the files are copied, you can make Student Disks for the students yourself, or tell students where to find the files so they can make their own Student Disks. Make sure the files get correctly copied by following the instructions in the Student Disks section above, which will ensure that students have enough disk space to complete all the tutorials, Tutorial Assignments, and Cases.

CTI SOFTWARE AND DATA FILES

You are granted a license to copy the Student Files to any computer or computer network used by students who have purchased this book. The files are included with the Instructor's Manual and may also be obtained electronically over the Internet. See the inside front or inside back cover of this book for more details.

A Tour of PowerPoint 7

Presentation to Potential Investors of Inca Imports International

CASE

Inca Imports International

Patricia Cuevas immigrated to the United States of America from San Salvador at the age of 12. After graduating from high school, she began working for Cisco Foods, a distributor to food-service businesses in the Los Angeles area. In the evenings, Patricia attended California State University at Northridge, where she earned a degree in Business Management. After 10 years with Cisco Foods, Patricia and another Cisco employee, Angelena Cristenas, began their own small business, Inca Imports International. Working with suppliers in South America, particularly in Ecuador and Peru, Patricia and Angelena imported fresh fruits and vegetables to North America during the winter and spring (which are summer and fall in South America) and sold them to small grocery stores in the Los Angeles area.

After three years in business, Inca Imports International has 34 employees and is healthy and growing. To promote further growth and profits, Patricia wants to establish a permanent distribution facility in Quito, Ecuador. This distribution facility, to include office and warehouse space, would allow Inca Imports International to maintain better quality control, shorten the time to market of the imported fruits and vegetables, and reduce costs.

As one of only three suppliers of imported fruits and vegetables in the entire Southern California area, Inca Imports International is in a position to increase the number of grocery stores and restaurant chains that purchase its goods and to increase the average order size. Besides building the facility in Ecuador, Patricia plans an aggressive marketing program that would significantly increase the cash flow and value of the rapidly growing company.

In an effort to obtain funding for the new distribution facility and marketing campaign, Patricia prepared a presentation that introduces Inca Imports International to potential investors. She has asked you to review her presentation, make changes to it, and print it.

Using the Tutorials Effectively

These tutorials will teach you to use PowerPoint 7 for Windows 95. The tutorials are designed to be used at a computer. Each tutorial is divided into sessions. Watch for the session headings, such as Session 1.1 and Session 1.2. It is a good idea to take a break between sessions. You will usually complete a session within 45 minutes, but take as much time as you need. Before you begin, read the following questions and answers. They are designed to help you use the tutorials effectively.

Where do I start?

Each tutorial begins with a case, which sets the scene for the tutorial and provides background information to help you understand what you will do in the tutorial. You can read the case before you go to the computer lab. In the lab, begin with Session 1.1.

How do I know what to do at the computer?

Each session contains steps that you will perform on the computer to learn how to use PowerPoint. Read the text that introduces each series of steps. The steps you need to do at a computer are numbered and have a colored background. Read each step carefully and completely before you try it.

How do I know if I did the step correctly?

As you work, compare your computer screen with the corresponding figure in the tutorial. Don't worry if your screen display is somewhat different from the figure. The important parts of the screen display are labeled in each figure. Just be sure these parts are on your screen.

What if I make a mistake?

Don't worry about making mistakes—that's part of the learning process. Paragraphs labeled "TROUBLE?" identify common problems and explain how to get back on track. Follow the steps in a TROUBLE? paragraph *only* if you are having the problem described. If you run into other problems, do the following:

- Carefully consider the current state of your system and any messages on the screen.
- Decide specifically what task you want to accomplish next.
- Determine how to accomplish the task, and then do it.

How do I use the Reference Windows?

Reference Windows summarize the procedures you learn in the tutorial steps. Don't do the steps in the Reference Window while you're working through the tutorial. Instead, use the Reference Windows when you work on the assignments at the end of the tutorial.

How can I test my understanding of what I learned in the tutorial?

At the end of each session, you can answer the Quick Check questions. The answers for the Quick Checks are at the end of the book.

After you have completed the entire tutorial, you can do the Tutorial Assignments and Cases. The Tutorial Assignments and Cases are carefully structured so you'll review what you've learned and then apply your knowledge to new situations.

What if I can't remember how to do something?

You can use the Task Reference at the end of the book; it is a table that summarizes the recommended method for accomplishing tasks. It also contains notes and cross references to Reference Windows for selected tasks. You can also use the index to locate information.

Now that you've learned how to use the tutorials effectively, you're ready to begin.

In this session you will learn how to start and exit PowerPoint, identify the parts of the PowerPoint window, and view a PowerPoint presentation. You will also learn some of the features of PowerPoint that will help you create effective presentations.

What Is PowerPoint?

PowerPoint is a powerful program that provides everything you need to produce an effective presentation in the form of black-and-white or color overheads, 35mm photographic slides, or on-screen slides. Using PowerPoint, you can prepare each component of your presentation: individual slides, speaker's notes, an outline of your presentation, and audience handouts. In addition, PowerPoint allows you to create a consistent format for each of these components and to manipulate text and add graphics to your presentations. You may have already seen your instructors use PowerPoint presentations to enhance their classroom lectures.

Presentation Slides, Masters, and Templates

Before you begin this tutorial, you need to understand several key PowerPoint terms: presentation, slide, master, and template. A **presentation** is a collection of slides, handouts, speaker's notes, and an outline, all together in one file. A **slide** is a single image or picture that is part of your visual presentation. Your presentation could include from one to dozens of slides. A **master** is a slide that contains the text and graphics that will appear on every slide of a particular kind in the presentation. For example, the company's name, the date, and the company's logo can be put on the slide master so this information will appear on every slide in the presentation. Using a slide master allows you to create a consistent appearance for your presentation. A **template** has a predefined format and color scheme that you can apply to your all of your presentation slides. PowerPoint includes a variety of professionally designed templates in a wide range of colors and styles.

Planning a Presentation

Planning a presentation before you create it improves the quality of your presentation, makes your presentation more effective and enjoyable, and, in the long run, saves you time and effort. As you plan your presentation, you should answer several questions. What is my purpose or objective for this presentation? What type of presentation is needed? Who is the audience? What information does that audience need? What is the physical location of my presentation? What is the best format for presenting the information contained in this presentation, given the location of the presentation?

In planning her presentation, Patricia answers these questions as follows:

- **Purpose for presentation:** To obtain funding

- **Type of presentation:** Sales presentation to sell expansion and marketing campaign ideas

- **Audience:** Potential investors, in their monthly board meeting or in a specially arranged meeting

- **Audience needs:** Company mission, profitability, and growth potential

- **Location of presentation:** A small boardroom with a computer, color monitor, and a projection system

- **Format:** Electronic slide show consisting of 7–10 slides and speaker's notes

Having planned her presentation, Patricia used PowerPoint to create it. Let's start PowerPoint and look at the first few slides of Patricia's presentation.

Starting PowerPoint

To use PowerPoint, you have to start (launch) the PowerPoint program. Let's do that now.

To start PowerPoint:

1. Make sure you have your formatted PowerPoint Student Disk.

   TROUBLE? If don't have a Student Disk, you need to get one. Your instructor will either give you one or ask you to make your own by following the steps outlined earlier in this tutorial in the section called "Creating Your Student Disk."

2. If necessary, turn on your computer. Windows 95 should start automatically, with the Start button in the lower- left corner of the screen. See Figure 1-1.

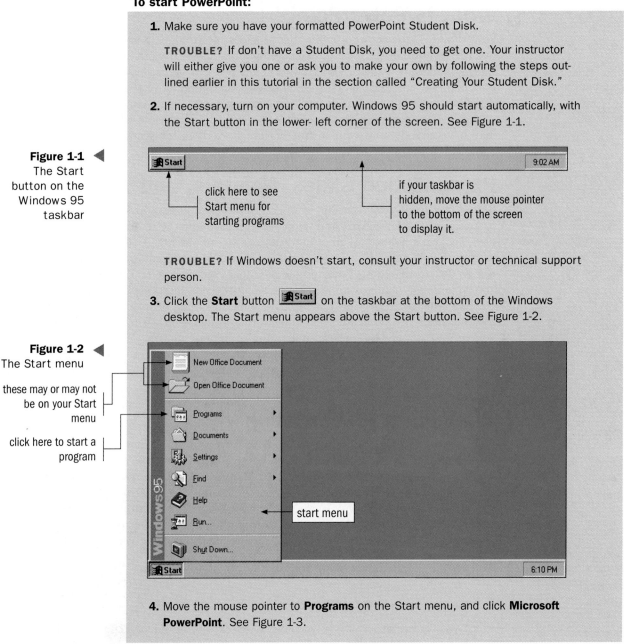

Figure 1-1 ◀
The Start
button on the
Windows 95
taskbar

click here to see
Start menu for
starting programs

if your taskbar is
hidden, move the mouse pointer
to the bottom of the screen
to display it.

   TROUBLE? If Windows doesn't start, consult your instructor or technical support person.

3. Click the **Start** button on the taskbar at the bottom of the Windows desktop. The Start menu appears above the Start button. See Figure 1-2.

Figure 1-2 ◀
The Start menu

these may or may not
be on your Start
menu

click here to start a
program

start menu

4. Move the mouse pointer to **Programs** on the Start menu, and click **Microsoft PowerPoint**. See Figure 1-3.

Figure 1-3 ◀
Starting the
PowerPoint
program

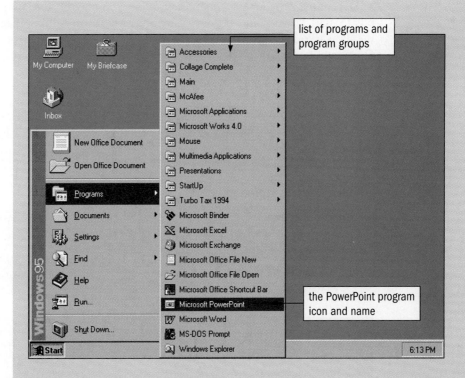

TROUBLE? If you don't see Microsoft PowerPoint, but you do see a program group called Microsoft Office or MSOffice, click on it, then click Microsoft PowerPoint.

TROUBLE? If you can't find PowerPoint on the Start menu, consult your instructor or technical support person.

After a moment or two, the PowerPoint startup dialog box appears on the screen. See Figure 1-4. PowerPoint is now running and ready to use.

Figure 1-4 ◀
The PowerPoint
window with the
PowerPoint
dialog box

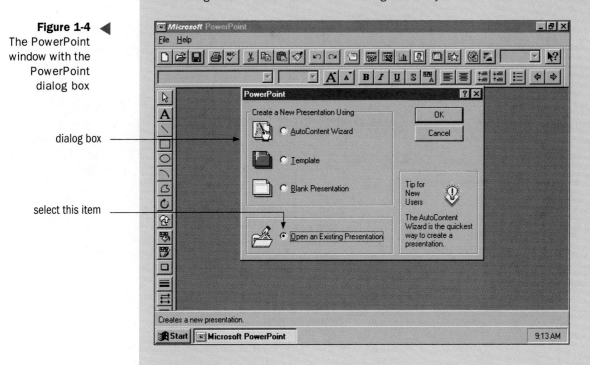

TROUBLE? A "Tip of the Day" dialog box might first appear in the PowerPoint window. If it does, click the OK button. A "What's New" or an other dialog box for first-time users might also appear. If it does, click the No or Close button.

Depending on your system configuration, you may be able to use several other methods to start PowerPoint. If your system has Microsoft Office 95 installed, you can click the PowerPoint icon on the Microsoft Office shortcut bar, or use the New Office Document or the Open Office Document on the Start menu to create or open Office files.

Opening an Existing Presentation

When you start PowerPoint, a startup dialog box appears on the screen. This dialog box contains several options. For example, it allows you to create a new presentation or to open an existing one.

Let's open the presentation that Patricia created for Inca Imports International.

To open Patricia's presentation:

1. Make sure the **Open an Existing Presentation** button in the PowerPoint startup dialog box is selected, as shown in Figure 1-4. If it isn't, click the **Open an Existing Presentation** button now.

2. Click the **OK** button. PowerPoint displays the File Open dialog box. See Figure 1-5.

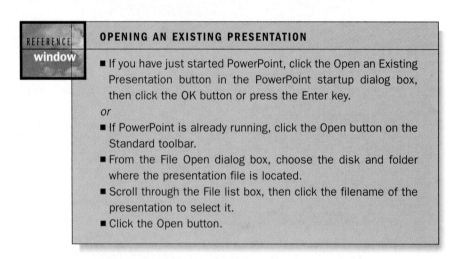

REFERENCE window

OPENING AN EXISTING PRESENTATION

- If you have just started PowerPoint, click the Open an Existing Presentation button in the PowerPoint startup dialog box, then click the OK button or press the Enter key.
  or
- If PowerPoint is already running, click the Open button on the Standard toolbar.
- From the File Open dialog box, choose the disk and folder where the presentation file is located.
- Scroll through the File list box, then click the filename of the presentation to select it.
- Click the Open button.

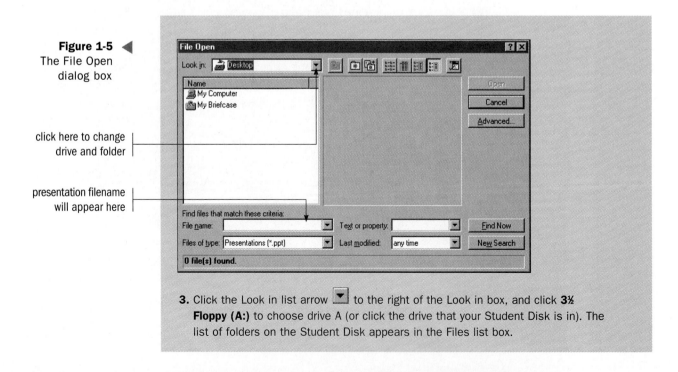

Figure 1-5 ◀
The File Open
dialog box

click here to change
drive and folder

presentation filename
will appear here

3. Click the Look in list arrow ▼ to the right of the Look in box, and click **3½ Floppy (A:)** to choose drive A (or click the drive that your Student Disk is in). The list of folders on the Student Disk appears in the Files list box.

TROUBLE? If you don't see any files or folders on the disk in drive A or if you get some other error, check to make sure that your Student Disk is in drive A. If you are using drive B, go back to Step 3 and select "B:" instead of "A:".

4. Double-click the **Tutorial.01** folder Tutorial 1 - Inca Imports to open the folder.

5. Click the name of the presentation file **Inca** in the Name list box.

TROUBLE? If the filename appears as Inca.ppt with the .ppt filename extension, don't worry. Some systems are configured to display filename extensions, and others are not.

6. Click the **Open** button. You can press the Enter key to execute a command in a dialog box that has a dark border around it. PowerPoint opens the presentation from the disk in the PowerPoint window. See Figure 1-6.

Figure 1-6 ◀
PowerPoint
window after
opening a
presentation

slide 1 of the
presentation

TROUBLE? If the presentation window contains text in an outline format instead of the slide view shown in the presentation window in Figure 1-6, click View on the menu bar near the top of the screen, and then click Slides.

TROUBLE? If the PowerPoint application window doesn't fill the entire monitor display, click the Maximize button in the upper-right corner of the PowerPoint window.

TROUBLE? If the filename appears in its own title bar instead of in the application title bar as shown in Figure 1-6, click the Maximize button in the presentation window.

You are now looking at slide 1 of Patricia's presentation.

TROUBLE? Depending on the resolution of your monitor and the configuration of your PowerPoint software, you may see more or less of the slide than what is shown in Figure 1-6. Don't worry if your view is slightly different.

Saving the Presentation with a New Name

To avoid accidentally overwriting the original disk file Inca, let's save the document using another filename. Saving the document with another filename creates a copy of the file that you can work with, leaving the original file unchanged should you need to revert to it.

To save the presentation with a new name:

1. Click **File** on the Menu bar, then click **Save As**. The Save As dialog box appears on the screen with the current filename highlighted in the File name text box.

2. In the File name box, edit the old filename (or type the new filename) **Intro to Inca Imports** in the File name text box.

3. Click the **Save** button. The Save As dialog box closes, and the new filename is displayed in the title bar at the top of the window.

Slide 1 of Patricia's presentation is displayed in the presentation window.

The PowerPoint Window

Let's examine the PowerPoint window, as shown in Figure 1-7. The PowerPoint window contains features common to all Windows applications, as well as features specific to PowerPoint.

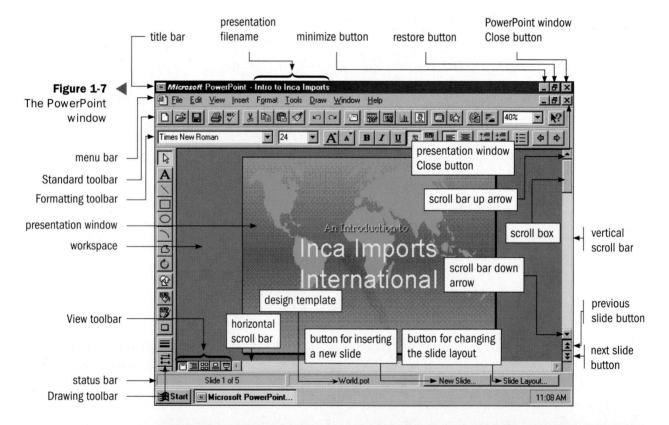

Figure 1-7
The PowerPoint window

Common Windows Elements

Several elements of the PowerPoint window are common to other Windows 95 applications. For example, the PowerPoint window has a menu bar, scroll bars, and a title bar. The title bar contains the Minimize, Maximize (or Restore), and Close buttons. These elements function the same way in PowerPoint as they do in other Windows applications.

The Scroll Bars

In PowerPoint, the vertical and horizontal scroll bars also function the same way they do in other Windows applications. The scroll arrows on the vertical scroll bar allow you to scroll the presentation window up or down; those on the horizontal scroll bar allow you to scroll the presentation window left or right. The scroll box (the square button on the scroll bars) allows you to quickly scroll to any location in the presentation. As you move the scroll box, PowerPoint displays a box telling you the slide number at the scroll position. Below the vertical scroll bar are the Previous Slide and Next Slide buttons. Clicking these buttons moves you to the previous or the next slide, respectively.

The Status Bar

The bottom bar of the PowerPoint window (which is just above the Windows 95 taskbar) is called the **status bar**. It tells you which slide you're working on, the design template for the current presentation, and, when you move the mouse pointer to a command button, provides a description of the command. The status bar also contains two shortcut buttons: the New Slide button and the Slide Layout button.

The Toolbars

Like many Windows 95 applications, PowerPoint supplies several toolbars, as shown in Figure 1-7. A **toolbar** is a horizontal or vertical ribbon of icons that provides menu shortcuts. When you move the mouse pointer over one of the buttons on the toolbar, you will see its **ToolTip**, or a yellow square containing the name of the button. You will learn to use the toolbars for tasks that are repeated often, such as opening or saving a file.

The toolbar immediately below the menu bar is the **Standard toolbar**, which allows you to use many of the standard Windows and PowerPoint commands, such as opening an existing presentation, saving your current presentation to disk, printing the presentation, and cutting and pasting text and graphics. Below the Standard toolbar is the **Formatting toolbar**, which allows you to format the text of your presentations. The vertical toolbar on the left edge of the PowerPoint window is the **Drawing toolbar**, which allows you to draw lines and shapes and enter text on your slides.

By using the Toolbars command feature on the View menu, you can turn off ToolTips, display buttons in a larger size, display other toolbars such as an additional drawing toolbar or the Microsoft toolbar, add new toolbars, or create a customized toolbar. You can also add buttons to a toolbar by choosing the Customize feature on the Toolbars menu.

As with other Windows applications, PowerPoint lets you select commands by using the pull-down menus with the keyboard or the mouse, by using shortcut keys, or by using buttons on a toolbar. Because the buttons on the toolbars are usually the easiest and fastest method of selecting commands, in these tutorials you will use the toolbars more often than the pull-down menus or keyboard.

The View Toolbar

The small toolbar immediately above the status bar is the **View toolbar**, which contains buttons that allow you to change the way you view a slide presentation. Each way of seeing a presentation is called a **view**, and the status bar indicates which view you are in. Clicking the **Slide View button** ▣ allows you to see and edit text and graphics on an individual slide. You are in Slide View now. You can click the **Outline View button** ▤ to see and edit your entire presentation in outline format. Clicking the **Slide Sorter View button** ▦ changes the view to miniature images of all the slides at once. You use this view to change the order of the slides or set special features for your slide show. Clicking the **Notes Pages View button** ▣ changes the view so you can see and edit your presentation notes on individual slides. To present your slide show, you can click the **Slide Show button** ▣. You can also change views by clicking View on the menu bar, then selecting the view you want. Let's practice these features next.

Previewing the Presentation and Changing the Slide Order

Patricia wants to see all of her slides at once to check their order. You will use the View toolbar to switch to Slide Sorter View to preview all of Patricia's slides on one screen, then use the Slide Sorter to change the order of the slides.

To view a presentation, or slide show, in Slide Sorter View:

1. Move the mouse pointer to the **Slide Sorter View** button ⊞ on the View toolbar, but don't click the mouse button yet. After a second or two, the ToolTip "Slide Sorter View" for this button appears.

2. Click the **Slide Sorter View** button ⊞. Your screen now looks like Figure 1-8.

Figure 1-8 ◄
Presentation in
Slide Sorter
View

selected slide (black
box around slide)

slide number

slide Sorter
View button

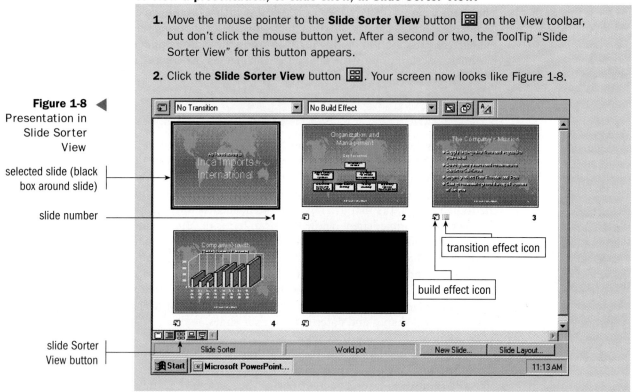

As you can see, each slide is shown in miniature. In the upper-left corner of the presentation window is slide 1, which is the title slide for Patricia's presentation. To the right is slide 2, which shows the company's organization and management chart. Slide 3 shows the mission statement of Inca Imports International. Slide 4 presents the company's gross income by quarter over a two-year period. Slide 5 is blank, to mark the end of the slide show. So far Patricia has created only five slides for her presentation.

At this point Patricia realizes that slide 3 (company's mission statement) should go before slide 2 (organization and management chart). Patricia would like you to use the Slide Sorter View to change the order of her slides.

To change the order of the slides:

1. Click slide 3 to select it. A heavy gray or black line appears around slide 3 to show you that it is selected.

2. Click and hold the mouse pointer on slide 3, then drag the mouse pointer between slides 1 and 2, but do not release the mouse button. The mouse pointer changes to 🖑. A thin vertical line shows the slide's new position. See Figure 1-9.

Figure 1-9 ◄
Moving a slide

mouse pointer ——

new position of slide ——

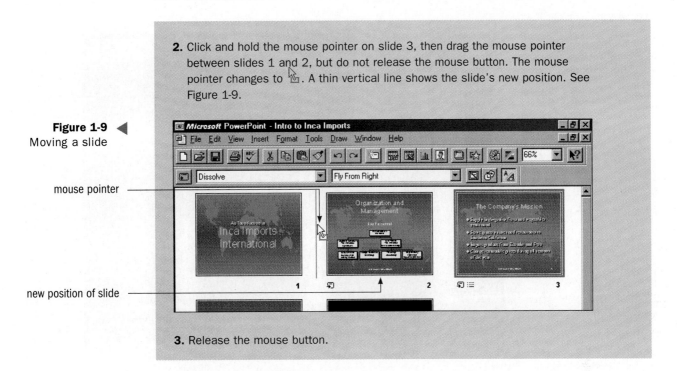

3. Release the mouse button.

You have successfully moved the mission statement slide to become slide 2 and the organizational chart to become slide 3.

Viewing the Presentation

You are now ready to view the slide show as it would be presented to potential investors. Right now Patricia's presentation has only five slides, but her completed presentation will have many more. Let's use the Slide Show button on the View toolbar to view Patricia's slide show.

To view the slide show:

1. Click slide 1 in the Slide Sorter View to make the first slide active in the Slide Sorter window. When you run a slide show, the first slide that appears on the screen is the slide that is selected; therefore, if you want to start the presentation at the beginning you have to select slide 1. To start the slide show from any other slide, just select that slide.

2. Click the **Slide Show** button 🖵 on the View toolbar.

TROUBLE? IIf you're not sure which button to click, move the mouse pointer to the buttons on the View toolbar and read the ToolTips.

The first slide fills the entire screen. See Figure 1-10. After reviewing slide 1, you're ready to advance to slide 2.

Figure 1-10 ◀
Slide 1 (title
slide) in Slide
Show View

3. Click the left mouse button or press the **spacebar**. Don't worry about the location of the mouse pointer. PowerPoint advances from slide 1 to slide 2. You will see only the title, "The Company's Mission," not the actual mission plan because Patricia made this a build slide. A **build slide** is a slide in which items in a list build one at a time as you click the left mouse button or press the **spacebar**.

4. Click the left mouse button or press the **spacebar**. The first item in the bulleted list, "Supply high-quality fruits and vegetables year-round," appears on the slide. Patricia has used a build effect called **Fly from right**, which, as you can see, causes the item to appear on the screen moving right to left.

5. Click the left mouse button or press the **spacebar**. Notice that the first item in the list changes color and the second item, "Serve grocery stores and restaurants in Southern California" flies onto the screen. See Figure 1-11.

Figure 1-11 ◀
Slide 2 with first
two builds

dimmed text ———

active build text ———

The Company's Mission

• Supply high-quality fruits and vegetables year-round
• Serve grocery stores and restaurants in Southern California

6. Click the left mouse button twice or press the **spacebar** twice to bring the last two items in the list of the company's mission onto the screen. You're now ready to advance the presentation to slide 3.

7. Click the left mouse button or press the **spacebar**. PowerPoint now displays the organization and management chart of Inca Imports International. Patricia created this organizational chart using **Microsoft Organization Chart**, a program that

comes with PowerPoint to make preparing charts for your presentation easier. Patricia is now ready to see slide 4.

8. Click the left mouse button or press the **spacebar**. PowerPoint displays slide 4, which is a chart showing Inca Imports' gross income over a two-year period. See Figure 1-12. Patricia created this chart by typing numbers into a table. PowerPoint automatically formatted and displayed the information in an attractive three-dimensional chart.

You might also notice that this slide has a **footer**, which contains information at the bottom of the slide that will appear on every slide (except the title slide and the blank slide at the end). In this case the footer contains the company name and the slide number.

Figure 1-12 ◀
Slide 4 with
PowerPoint
chart

slide title

chart

footer

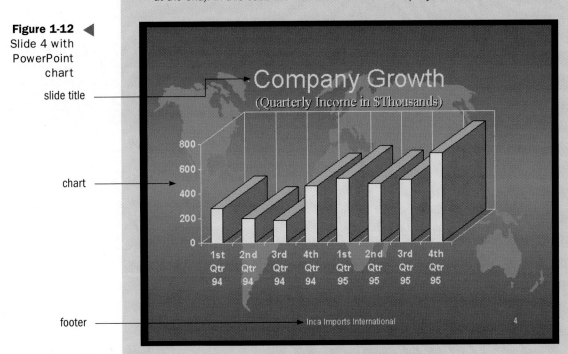

9. Click the left mouse button twice or press the **spacebar** twice, once to display the blank slide that tells Patricia she's at the end of her presentation, and a second time to return to the Slide Sorter View of PowerPoint.

As you can see, Patricia has created an attractive, effective slide presentation. By using PowerPoint's many features, you will create presentations like this one with minimum effort and maximum efficiency.

Saving the Modified Presentation

Now that you have changed the order of the slides and previewed the presentation, Patricia is satisfied with the results of your work for now and asks you to save the presentation to your disk. She will view other parts of the presentation (for example, speaker's notes) and ask you to print the presentation in the next session. You must remember to save a presentation after you complete it, even if you've saved it one or more times while you were creating it. It's also a good idea to save your presentation before printing it. Let's save the presentation now.

To save a presentation to your disk:

1. Make sure the Student Disk is still in drive A. Because you changed the order of the slides, this is a good time to save the revised version of the slide presentation. You will use the current (default) filename.

> **2.** Click the **Save** button 🖫 on the Standard toolbar. PowerPoint saves your presentation using the current filename, Intro to Inca Imports.

Quick Check

1 In one to three sentences, describe the purpose of the PowerPoint program and what you can do with it.

2 Define the following terms:
   a. PowerPoint presentation
   b. slide master
   c. template

3 What are the six questions you should ask in planning a presentation?

4 Describe how you started PowerPoint on your computer system.

5 How do you open an existing presentation in PowerPoint?

6 How do you save a presentation using a different filename?

7 Define the following terms:
   a. status bar
   b. ToolTip
   c. Standard toolbar
   d. Formatting toolbar
   e. View toolbar
   f. build slide

8 Describe the following views of a presentation:
   a. Slide View
   b. Slide Sorter View
   c. Slide Show View

9 In Slide Show View, how do you advance to the next slide? How do you go back to the previous slide?

This concludes Session 1.1. You can exit PowerPoint or continue to the next session. If you desire to exit PowerPoint, click the Close button ☒ on the title bar in the upper-right corner of the PowerPoint window or click File, then click Exit.

SESSION 1.2

In this session you will learn how to view the presentation in Outline View and in Speaker's Notes View. You will also learn how to print a presentation and how to use the PowerPoint Help feature.

If you exited PowerPoint at the end of the previous session, you should start PowerPoint again and open the presentation called "Intro to Inca Imports."

Viewing the Outline and Speaker's Notes

A presentation includes much more than just slides. It can also include an outline, speaker's notes, and handouts. Let's view the presentation outline and speaker's notes. (**Handouts** are simply printouts of the slides, with two, three, or six slides printed on each page.)

To view the presentation Outline and the Speaker's Notes:

1. Click the **Outline View** button ▤ on the View toolbar. PowerPoint displays the outline of the presentation, and the Outlining toolbar appears vertically on the left side of the window. See Figure 1-13. The outline is always in black type, even if your presentation is in color.

Figure 1-13 ◄
Presentation window in Outline View

slide number

slide icon (selected slide)

slide icon (not selected)

outlining toolbar

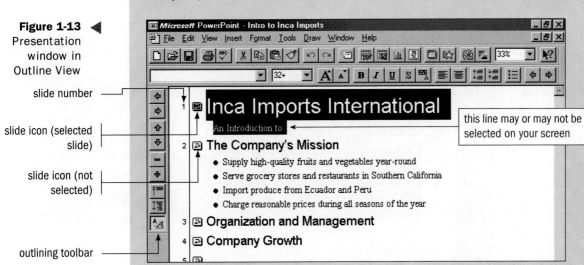

this line may or may not be selected on your screen

With the outline on the screen, you can edit the text of the slides, just as you would edit text with a word processor. The changes you make to the outline will automatically appear on the slide images. You can also use the Outline View to create text for your slides.

TROUBLE? If slide 1 isn't selected as shown in Figure 1-13, click the slide icon to the right of the slide number at the beginning of the outline.

2. Click the **Notes Pages View** button ▣ on the View toolbar. PowerPoint displays a note page, which includes a copy of the slide at the top of the page and space for speaker's notes at the bottom of the page. You can use PowerPoint to create, edit, and print notes for slides. Let's set the page zoom to 100% so we can read the text of the notes.

3. Click **View**, click **Zoom**, then click the **100%** button in the Zoom dialog box, and click the **OK** button.

You should see the notes for slide 1. See Figure 1-14.

Figure 1-14 ◄
Slide 1 in Note Pages View

slide

speaker's notes

Note Pages View button

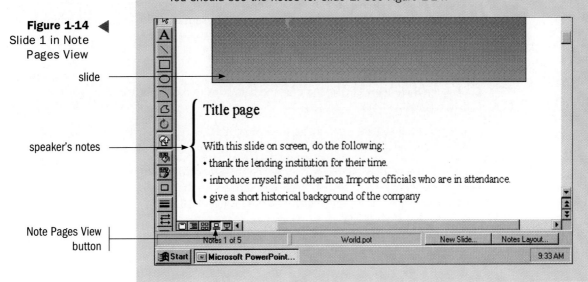

TROUBLE? If you can't see the entire text on the notes page, drag the scroll box in the vertical scroll bar until you can see all the text.

After you read the notes for slide 1, you are ready to go on to slide 2. Let's use the scroll box to select slide 2.

4. Drag the **scroll box** about a third of the way down the scroll bar, but don't release the mouse button. As you drag the scroll box, PowerPoint displays the ScrollTip with slide number and title next to the mouse pointer on the scroll bar. See Figure 1-15.

Figure 1-15 ◀
Using the scroll box to change slides

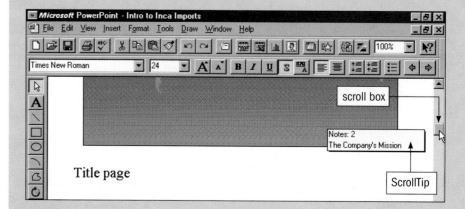

5. Release the mouse button when the scroll box reaches "Notes 2." Scroll the presentation window until you can read the notes at the bottom of the slide.

6. Click the **Next Slide** button ⬇ at the bottom of the vertical scroll bar. PowerPoint displays slide 3. Scroll the presentation window again as necessary to view all the notes

7. Continue going through the slides, one at a time, to read the speaker's notes.

Viewing the Presentation in Black-and-White View

Because you don't have a color printer, and Patricia created her slides in color, you will need to preview Patricia's presentation in black and white before printing it for her. Some presentation designs look great in color, but they are not legible when viewed or printed in black and white. Let's view the Inca Imports presentation in black and white before printing it.

To view the presentation in Black-and-White View:

1. Click the **Slide View** button and drag the scroll box to the top of the scroll bar to view slide 1.

   TROUBLE? If you are still viewing the slides at 100%, you can click View, then click Zoom, and select "fit." You should now see each slide in its entirety.

2. Click the **B&W View** button 🔲 located on the Standard toolbar near the top of the PowerPoint window. A Color View box appears on the screen to remind you of what each slide looks like in color view. See Figure 1-16.

Figure 1-16 ◀
Presentation
window in
Black-and-
White View

Color View window

black-and-white
presentation window

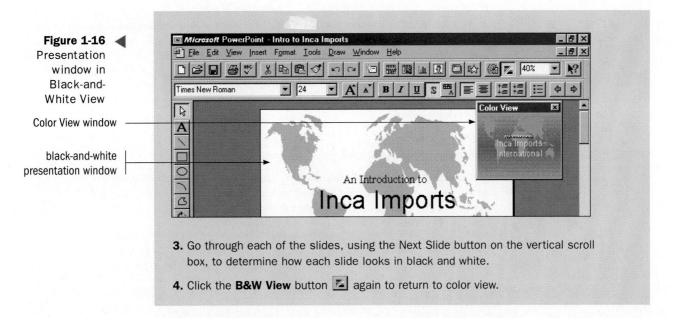

3. Go through each of the slides, using the Next Slide button on the vertical scroll box, to determine how each slide looks in black and white.

4. Click the **B&W View** button ▣ again to return to color view.

All of the slides are legible in black and white, so you don't have to make any adjustments to the design before printing the presentation. We will print the presentation next.

Printing the Presentation

Patricia would like to keep a printout (or "hard copy") of her presentation for her records. You will need to print the presentation for Patricia.

To print the presentation:

1. Click **File**, then click **Print** to display the Print dialog box. See Figure 1-17.

Figure 1-17 ◀
Print dialog box

type the range here

select this to print
range of slides

make sure this is
selected

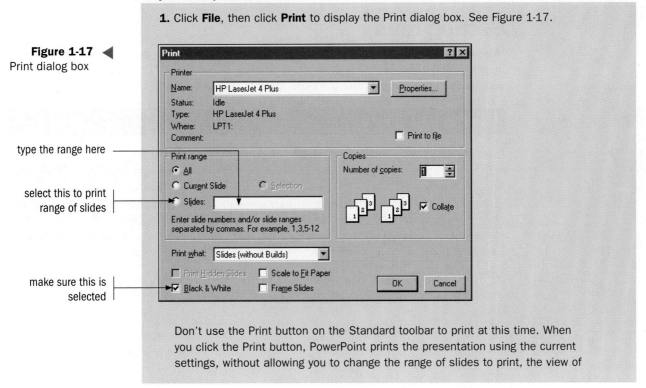

Don't use the Print button on the Standard toolbar to print at this time. When you click the Print button, PowerPoint prints the presentation using the current settings, without allowing you to change the range of slides to print, the view of the output, or other settings. However, you can use the Print button to print when you know the print settings are correct. To print the slides, you can be in any view except Slide Show View.

2. Make sure **Slides (without Builds)** is selected in the Print what box. You don't want the blank slide at the end of the presentation printed, so you'll only print slides 1 through 4.

3. In the Print range box, click the **Slides** button. The insertion point will move to the Slides text box. Type **1-4**.

4. If you're using a black-and-white printer, make sure the **Black & White** check box at the lower left of the dialog box is checked. If you are using a color printer, do not check this box so your slides will print in color.

5. Click the **OK** button to print the slides. Be patient. Graphics usually take a long time to print, even on a relatively fast printer. The slides are printed one slide per page. After giving your printouts to Patricia, she asks you to print the outline as well. After you finish printing the slides, you are ready to print the outline and notes pages.

6. Click **File** then click **Print**.

7. Click the Print what list arrow ▼ in the Print what text box, scroll down the list to select **Outline View**, then click the **OK** button.

   Patricia would also like to have a printout of her speaker's notes.

8. Repeat Steps 6 and 7, only this time select **Notes Pages** in the Print what list box.

You can now give Patricia printouts of her complete presentation.

Getting Help

When you're using PowerPoint, how do you know which button to click or which menu item to select? The best way is to practice using PowerPoint. The tutorials in this book will give you the training and the experience you need to utilize PowerPoint to its fullest.

Using the Help Index

Even the most experienced PowerPoint user needs help every now and then. If you need help using or executing a command in PowerPoint you can always consult the Help and Wizard features. First, let's review some aspects of the Help feature.

After you click Help on the menu bar, you can choose several ways of accessing the Help information. When you click Microsoft PowerPoint Help Topics, the Help Topics window appears on the screen, as shown in Figure 1-18. You can click on one of the four folder tabs at the top of the window to find information about PowerPoint commands and features:

Figure 1-18
Help Topics:
Microsoft
Power Point
dialog box

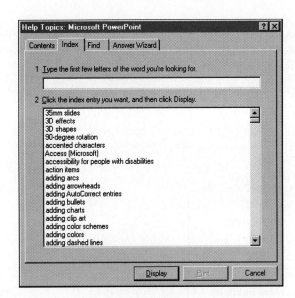

Clicking the **Contents** folder tab lets you choose one of a few broad topics about which you'd like to learn more.

Clicking the **Index** folder tab lets you choose a word from an alphabetized list of topics.

Clicking the **Find** folder tab lets you search for words and phrases in help topics, instead of searching for information by category.

Clicking the **Answer Wizard** folder tab starts the Answer Wizard to answer "How do I?" and "Tell me about" questions. In some cases, the Answer Wizard may help you complete certain tasks by walking you through the necessary steps. You may also access the Answer Wizard by clicking Help on the menu bar, then clicking Answer Wizard.

Let's use the Help Index to learn how to create an organizational chart.

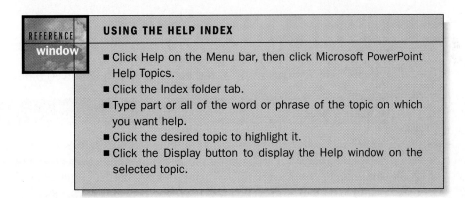

REFERENCE
window

USING THE HELP INDEX

- Click Help on the Menu bar, then click Microsoft PowerPoint Help Topics.
- Click the Index folder tab.
- Type part or all of the word or phrase of the topic on which you want help.
- Click the desired topic to highlight it.
- Click the Display button to display the Help window on the selected topic.

To search for help on a specific topic:

1. Click **Help** on the Menu bar, then click **Microsoft PowerPoint Help Topics**. PowerPoint displays the Help Topics dialog box.

2. If necessary, click the **Index** tab to bring it to the front.

3. With the cursor in the text box at the top of the Help Topics dialog box, type **organiz**, the first few letters of "organization chart," the topic on which you want help. As you type, you will notice that "Organization Chart" becomes highlighted in the list of topics. You can type as few or as many letters of a word as you need when you get help.

4. Click the **Display** button in the Help Topics dialog box. Now PowerPoint displays the Topics Found dialog box, with a list of help topics associated with organizational charts.

5. In the Topics Found dialog box, click **Insert an organizational chart** and then click the **Display** button to tell Help to show that topic.

PowerPoint now displays a window that describes how to insert an organizational chart into a presentation. See Figure 1-19.

Figure 1-19 ◀
PowerPoint
Help window

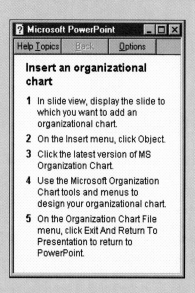

6. After you read the information in the Microsoft PowerPoint Help window, click the **Close** button ⊠ in the upper-right corner of the Help window.

The PowerPoint Help window disappears from the screen. By knowing (or guessing) one or more words that describe a feature on which you want help, you can use the Index feature to find virtually any information about using PowerPoint.

Using Context-Sensitive Help

Another method for getting help in PowerPoint is to use the Help button 🔘 on the Standard toolbar. The Help button provides **context-sensitive help**, that is, help about a specific part of PowerPoint. When you click the Help button and then click any feature within the PowerPoint window or click a pull-down menu command, PowerPoint instantly provides help for you on that feature or command. For example, let's get help on the Insert Graph button 📊.

To get help on the Insert Graph button:

1. Click the **Help** button 🔘 on the Standard toolbar. The mouse pointer becomes ▯. Now, whatever screen element you click or whatever menu command you select, PowerPoint will give you help on that feature or command.

2. Click the **Insert Graph** button 📊 on the Standard toolbar. PowerPoint displays a brief description of the button. See Figure 1-20.

Figure 1-20
Context-
sensitive help

help window

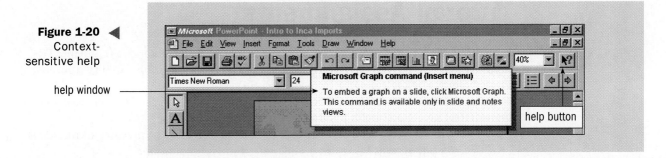

help button

After reading the description of the button, click the left mouse button to clear the box. Feel free to explore the other methods of getting help in the Help Topics window now, and then in the future use these methods as necessary for getting help in PowerPoint.

Exiting PowerPoint

Now that you are finished viewing and printing Patricia's presentation, you can exit PowerPoint.

To exit PowerPoint:

1. Click **File** on the menu bar, then click **Exit**. You could also click the Close button in the upper-right corner of the PowerPoint window. PowerPoint may display a dialog box with the message "Save changes to Intro to Inca Imports?" This message indicates that you have modified the document since last saving it and that you probably need to save it again before exiting.

2. If the "Save changes" message appeared, click the **Yes** button to save the current version and exit PowerPoint.

You have exited PowerPoint, and you should now see the Windows desktop on your screen. You can now shut down your computer, or use other programs.

Quick Check

1 Describe the purpose of the following:
   a. Outline View
   b. Note Pages View

2 What is the purpose of previewing a color presentation in black and white?

3 Describe how you would print the slides and the speaker's notes of a presentation.

4 How would you find information about inserting clip art in PowerPoint?

5 What is the easiest way to get information on an item that appears in the PowerPoint window?

6 Using the Help feature in PowerPoint, define or describe the following:
   a. Design Templates
   b. the Format Painter
   c. transitions

Tutorial Assignments

In the following Tutorial Assignments, make sure you click the Open an Existing File button when you start PowerPoint (or click the Open button on the Standard toolbar if PowerPoint is already running) to open each file.

Open the file Health from the Tutorial Assignments folder on the Student Disk and immediately save it as Health Insurance. Then do the following:

1. Use the View toolbar to switch to Slide Sorter View to preview all the slides on one screen. How many slides are in the presentation?
2. Use the Slide Sorter View to change slide 3 to slide 2.
3. View the slide show. What is the subject of slide 4?
4. Switch to Notes Pages View.
5. Zoom the notes pages to 100%, then view the notes for all the slides. Which slide has speaker's notes that explain what the basic care option emphasizes?
6. Drag the scroll box to move to slide 7. What is the purpose of this slide?
7. Use the Next Slide button to go to slide 8. Which month is open enrollment for the health care options?
8. Delete slide 6. *Hint:* Use the Help feature to find out how to delete a slide.
9. Save the presentation using the current filename, "Health Insurance."

10. Print slide 1 only. *Note:* In the Print dialog box, select Slide (without Builds).
11. Print the Notes Page for slide 2 only.
12. Using Help, search for help on "build slide." What is a build slide? Which slides in this presentation are build slides?

13. Search for help on "transitions." What is a transition? Which slides in this presentation have a transition?
14. Using the Help Index, look up ClipArt Gallery. In your own words, what is the ClipArt Gallery? Which slides in this presentation include a clip art image?
15. From the Help menu, click the Tip of the Day. What does it say?
16. Close the presentation file.

Case Problem

1. RSVP Consultants, Inc. Meryl and Albert Szajnberg own RSVP Consultants, Inc., a wedding and special-events consulting company. RSVP's goals include building a new reception center, training five new consultants, and winning the bid to host a local Chamber of Commerce summer celebration.

1. What would be the purpose of an RSVP presentation to each of the following audiences? In your answer, mention the kind of information each audience would need to know.
   a. investors
   b. RSVP's new employees
   c. potential clients

2. Select the type of presentation (recommending a strategy, selling a service or product, providing training, and so forth) RSVP would create for each audience listed in Question 1. *Hint:* Use Help to look at the items in the AutoContent Wizard.
3. Identify a likely location (boardroom, auditorium, classroom, or other location) for each of the three presentations listed in Question 1.
4. Select a format (overhead, paper, 35mm slides, or on-screen) for each presentation. Next, open the file RSVP from the Case Assignments folder on the Student Disk and immediately save it as Case 1 – RSVP Services; do the following:
5. Switch to Slide Sorter View to preview all the slides. How many slides are in the presentation?

6. Move slide 6 to slide 5 in Slide Sorter View.
7. View the slide show from beginning to end.
8. Indicate which slides would be appropriate for training new employees.
9. Indicate which slides would be appropriate for selling RSVP's services to a prospective client.

10. Describe how to hide a slide within a presentation. (*Hint:* Use the Help feature to learn about hidden slides.) How would this feature be helpful in using the current presentation for clients only?
11. Switch to Notes Pages View and read the speaker's notes for all the slides. Which slide notes have the word "client" or "clients"?
12. Print the Notes Page for slide 9.
13. Save the presentation using the current filename, "Case 1 - RSVP Services."
14. Print slide 7 only. Note: In the Print dialog box, select Slide (without Builds).
15. What is WordArt? When would you use it? *Hint:* Use the Help Index to look up this topic.
16. Close the presentation.

Creating a Text Slide Show

Presentation to Reach Potential Customers of Inca Imports International

CASE

Market Research

Following Patricia Cuevas's successful presentation to potential investors, Inca Imports International received a collateral commitment from Commercial Financial Bank of Southern California. The commitment secured debt financing for up to $1.5 million to begin construction of a distribution facility in Quito, Ecuador, and to launch a marketing campaign to allow Inca Imports to position itself for further expansion.

Patricia assigned Carl Vetterli, Vice President of Sales and Marketing, the task of identifying potential customers and developing methods to reach them. Carl has scheduled a meeting with Patricia, Angelena Cristenas (Vice President of Operations), Enrique Hoffmann (Director of Marketing), and others to review the results of his market research. His presentation will include a demographic profile of Inca Imports' current customers and the results from a customer satisfaction survey, a vision statement of the company's future growth, a list of options for attracting new clients, and recommendations for a marketing strategy.

In this tutorial, you will create some of Carl's slides for his presentation.

In this session you will learn how to use the AutoContent Wizard to create an outline and how to use Outline View to insert and edit text in an outline.

Planning the Presentation

Before starting PowerPoint, Carl identifies the purpose of and audience for his presentation.

- **Purpose of the presentation:** To identify potential customers and ways to reach them

- **Type of presentation:** Recommend a strategy for the new marketing campaign

- **Audience for the presentation:** Patricia, Angelena, Enrique, and other key staff members in a weekly executive meeting

- **Audience needs:** To understand who our current clients are and to determine the best way to reach similar new clients

- **Location of the presentation:** Small boardroom

- **Format:** Oral presentation; electronic slide show of five to seven slides

Now that Carl has planned his presentation, you can use PowerPoint to create it.

Using the AutoContent Wizard to Create an Outline

PowerPoint helps you create effective presentations by using wizards. A **wizard** asks you a series of questions to determine the organizational structure and style for your presentation. By using the **AutoContent Wizard**, you can choose a presentation category such as "Selling a Product, Service, or an Idea," "Recommending a Strategy," or "General." After you have selected the type of presentation you want, the AutoContent Wizard creates a general outline for you to follow.

If you open a new presentation without using the AutoContent Wizard, you must create your own outline, one slide at a time. Creating your own outline is appropriate and effective if it doesn't fall into one of PowerPoint's predefined types. Carl, however, wants you to use the AutoContent Wizard to create his slides quickly because his presentation topic is a common one: recommending a strategy. The AutoContent Wizard will allow you to create a title slide and select a standard outline to guide you in creating his presentation. Let's start PowerPoint and use the AutoContent Wizard.

To start PowerPoint with the AutoContent Wizard:

1. If necessary, start PowerPoint.

2. When the startup dialog box appears, click the **AutoContent Wizard** button in the PowerPoint startup dialog box. See Figure 2-1.

Figure 2-1 ◄
PowerPoint
startup
dialog box

TROUBLE? If the PowerPoint startup dialog box doesn't appear on your screen, click File, then click New. When the New Presentation dialog box appears on the screen, make sure the Presentations tab is selected, then click the AutoContent Wizard button, and click the OK button.

3. Click the **OK** button to open the first of six AutoContent Wizard dialog boxes. The first dialog box provides information about the function of the AutoContent Wizard.

4. Read the information in the AutoContent Wizard dialog box, then click the **Next** button at the bottom of the dialog box. The next dialog box of the AutoContent Wizard appears on the screen. This dialog box creates a title slide for your presentation. The insertion point in the text box labeled "What is your name?" indicates that text will appear at this point when you start typing.

   TROUBLE? If the insertion point appears in the text box labeled "What are you going to talk about?" hold down the Shift key and then press the Tab key to move the insertion point to the name box. If there is already a name entered in the "What is your name?" text box, press Shift+Tab to highlight the text so you can replace it in the next step.

5. Type **Carl Vetterli**, then press the **Tab** key. The name you typed appears in the first text box, and the insertion point moves to the second text box, labeled "What are you going to talk about?"

6. Type **Reaching Potential Customers**, press the **Tab** key to move the insertion point to the next text box labeled, "Other information you'd like to display?", and type **Inca Imports International**. See Figure 2-2.

Figure 2-2 ◄
Second
dialog box of
Auto-Content
Wizard

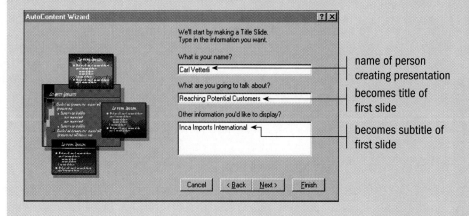

TROUBLE? If you accidentally pressed the Enter key before typing all the data, click the Back button in the next dialog box to return to the previous dialog box, click the pointer in the empty text box, and continue entering the above information.

7. Click the **Next** button to move to the next step of the AutoContent Wizard. This dialog box provides six standard formats or outlines for a presentation. Carl wants to recommend a marketing strategy for reaching potential customers.

8. Click the **Recommending a Strategy** button. Notice that the summary on the right gives a description of the content of the Recommending a Strategy presentation. See Figure 2-3.

Figure 2-3
Third dialog box of AutoContent Wizard

select this type of presentation

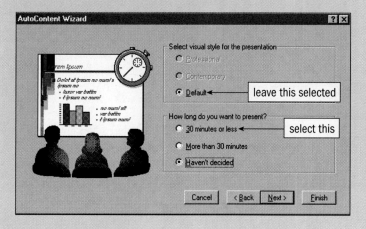

So far in the AutoContent Wizard, you have given Carl's presentation a title and subtitle and selected a type of outline (Recommending a Strategy).

Next, you will select the visual style, length, and mode of presentation.

To complete the AutoContent Wizard:

1. Click the **Next** button to move to the next step of the AutoContent Wizard. See Figure 2-4. This dialog box lets you choose a visual style and an approximate length for your presentation. Because Carl has scheduled a half-hour meeting, he wants the slide presentation to last about 20 minutes.

Figure 2-4
Fourth dialog box of AutoContent Wizard

2. If necessary, click the **Default** button to choose the default visual style. Then click the **30 minutes or less** button.

3. Click the **Next** button to move to the next step of the AutoContent Wizard. See Figure 2-5. This dialog box lets you choose which type of output you will use and whether you will print handouts. Carl will give an on-screen presentation, but he also wants to print his presentation as handouts to have a hard copy for his records.

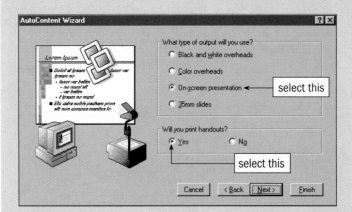

Figure 2-5 ◀
Fifth dialog box of AutoContent Wizard

4. If necessary, click the **On-screen presentation** button and the **Yes** button, so the dialog box looks like Figure 2-5.

5. Click the **Next** button, read the information in the dialog box, and then click the **Finish** button. PowerPoint now displays the first slide of the presentation. See Figure 2-6.

Figure 2-6 ◀
Title slide of presentation

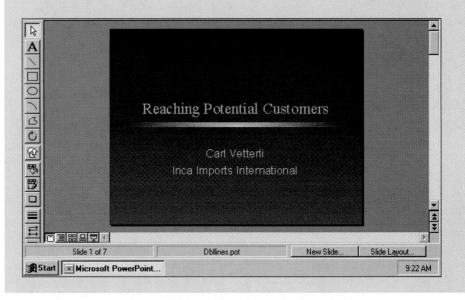

The AutoContent Wizard is now complete. Next you will adapt PowerPoint's default outline to fit Carl's presentation.

Adapting an AutoContent Outline

After Carl completes the AutoContent Wizard, PowerPoint displays Carl's title slide (slide 1) with his name and presentation title already filled in, as shown in Figure 2-6. In addition, PowerPoint creates additional slides with suggested text located in placeholders. A **placeholder** is a region of a slide reserved for inserting text or graphics. To adapt the AutoContent slides to your own presentation, you **select**, or highlight, the placeholders, one at a time, and then replace them with your own text. Because Outline View allows you to see the text of your presentation as a whole rather than as individual slides, Outline View is usually the easiest view for working with text. You can also apply formatting changes to the text and change the order of the slides in Outline View, just as you can in other views.

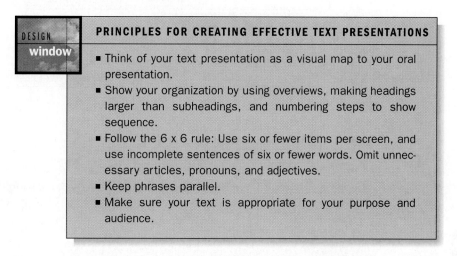

DESIGN
window

PRINCIPLES FOR CREATING EFFECTIVE TEXT PRESENTATIONS

- Think of your text presentation as a visual map to your oral presentation.
- Show your organization by using overviews, making headings larger than subheadings, and numbering steps to show sequence.
- Follow the 6 x 6 rule: Use six or fewer items per screen, and use incomplete sentences of six or fewer words. Omit unnecessary articles, pronouns, and adjectives.
- Keep phrases parallel.
- Make sure your text is appropriate for your purpose and audience.

In Outline View, each main heading of the outline, or the **title** of each slide, appears to the right of the slide icon and slide number, as shown in Figure 2-7. On the text slides, the subheadings, or the **main text** of each slide, are indented and bulleted under the title. PowerPoint can display just the titles of the slides or the entire outline with titles and main text.

To see the presentation in Outline View and display the slide titles only:

1. Click the **Outline View** button 📄 on the View toolbar to display the outline of the AutoContent slides, and display the Outlining toolbar. See Figure 2-7.

Slide number

Figure 2-7 ◀
Presentation in
Outline View

slide icon

show Titles button

Show All button

outlining toolbar

outline View selected

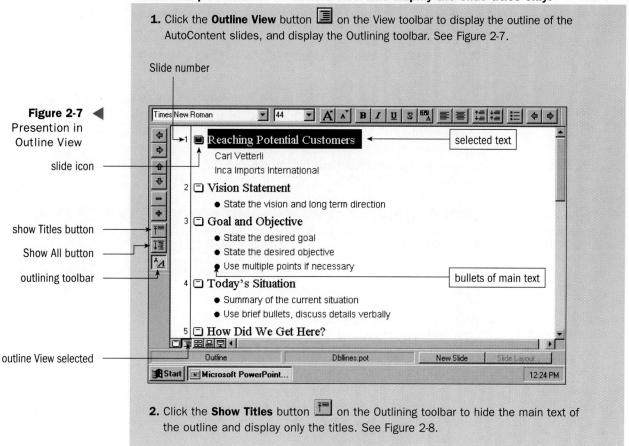

2. Click the **Show Titles** button 📄 on the Outlining toolbar to hide the main text of the outline and display only the titles. See Figure 2-8.

Figure 2-8 ◄
Outline View

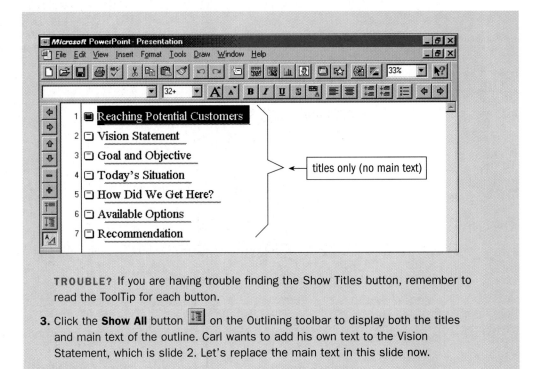

TROUBLE? If you are having trouble finding the Show Titles button, remember to read the ToolTip for each button.

3. Click the **Show All** button 📇 on the Outlining toolbar to display both the titles and main text of the outline. Carl wants to add his own text to the Vision Statement, which is slide 2. Let's replace the main text in this slide now.

To replace the main text in a slide:

1. Make sure the presentation window is maximized, if necessary, by clicking the **Maximize** button 🗖. (Your presentation window may already be maximized.) If necessary, drag the horizontal scroll button to the far left so you can see the left edge of the outline text.

2. Position the pointer on the bullet that is located just beneath the title of slide 2. The pointer changes to ✛.

3. Click ✛ on the bullet to select the text. See Figure 2-9. By clicking a bullet, you can quickly select all the text in a bulleted item of the main text of a slide. You could also select the text by positioning I before the "S" in the sentence "State the vision and long term direction" and dragging I over the text while holding down the mouse button. Once the text is selected, you can just start typing to replace it.

Figure 2-9 ◄
Outline after
selecting item

mouse pointer ——

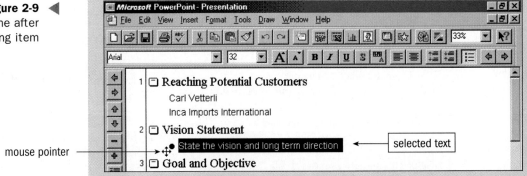

4. Type **Inca can improve the quality of its produce**. Your screen should now look like Figure 2-10. Notice that as soon as you started typing, the selected text disappeared as you typed the new phrase.

Figure 2-10
New text
in outline

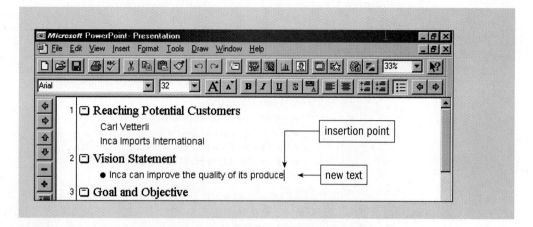

Carl has two more bullets he wants you to add to the Vision Statement slide. Let's do that now.

To add new text to the outline:

1. With the insertion point at the location shown in Figure 2-10, press the **Enter** key. When you press the Enter key, PowerPoint automatically inserts a bullet for the next item in the list, and the insertion point appears to the right of the bullet.

2. Type **Inca can sell more produce to more customers**, then press the **Enter** key.

3. Type **Inca can become the clear market leader in Southern California**, then press the **Enter** key. Your screen should now look like Figure 2-11.

Figure 2-11
Outline after
inserting text

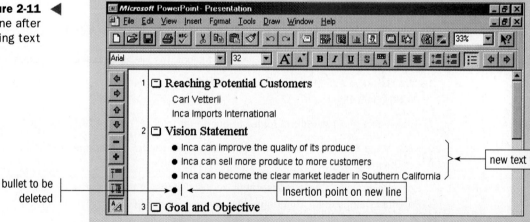

Carl realizes that he really wants only three items in the list, not four, so he asks you to delete the fourth bullet.

4. Press the **Backspace** key to delete the fourth bullet and move the insertion point to the end of the preceding line. Next Carl wants you to replace the placeholder text in slide 3, "Goal and Objective."

5. Make the changes to slide 3 using the text shown in Figure 2-12.

Figure 2-12
Outline after
inserting
text to slide 3

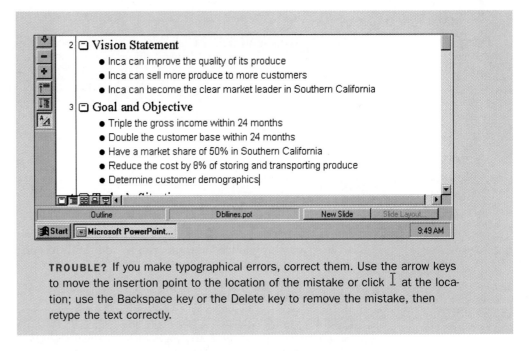

TROUBLE? If you make typographical errors, correct them. Use the arrow keys to move the insertion point to the location of the mistake or click I at the location; use the Backspace key or the Delete key to remove the mistake, then retype the text correctly.

Your presentation window should now look like Figure 2-12.

Saving the Presentation for the First Time

You have made substantial progress on Carl's presentation, and he asks you to save the changes.

To save a presentation for the first time:

1. Insert your Student Disk in drive A.

2. Click the **Save** button 🖫 on the Standard toolbar. The File Save dialog box opens.

3. Click the Save in list arrow, then click **3½ Floppy (A:)** (or whichever drive contains your Student Disk).

4. Double-click the **Tutorial.02 folder** to open that folder.

5. Click in the **File name** text box, type **Reaching Potential Customers**, and click the **Save** button.

PowerPoint saves Carl's presentation to the disk using the filename "Reaching Potential Customers." That name now appears in the Slide window title bar.

Quick Check

1 Describe the purpose of the AutoContent Wizard.

2 What is a disadvantage of the AutoContent Wizard over typing an outline from scratch?

3 Define each of the following:
a. placeholder
b. selecting text, a placeholder, or a slide
c. title (on a slide)
d. main text (on a slide)

4 Explain how to do the following:
a. Delete text in Outline View
b. Switch between Outline View and Slide View

5 How do you display only the slide titles in Outline View?

6 What is the 6 × 6 rule?

7 How do you select the text of a placeholder in Outline View?

This concludes Session 2.1. You can exit PowerPoint or continue to the next session.

SESSION

2.2

In this session, you'll learn more about using Outline View to edit and change text. If you exited PowerPoint at the end of the previous session, start the program again, open the presentation file "Reaching Potential Customers" from your Student Disk, and select Outline View.

Editing the Presentation in Outline View

As Carl reviews the text of the first three slides, he realizes that in a slide presentation, each text item should be as short as possible. It's easier for the audience to read short phrases. In addition, he knows that he'll be conveying most of the information orally, so the main text doesn't have to be complete sentences.

Carl decides to apply the 6 × 6 rule as much as possible and simplify the text in slide 2. Because the audience will be aware that Carl is talking about Inca Imports International, the company name is unnecessary. Similarly, articles ("the," "a"), many possessive pronouns ("your," "its"), and most adjectives ("high," "clear," "very") can safely be left out of titles and the main text. Therefore, Carl decides to change "Inca can improve the quality of its produce" to "Improve quality of produce." Carl also realizes that by changing the title of slide 3 from "Goal and Objective," to "Two-Year Goals," he can delete the words "within 24 months" from the bulleted list.

To edit the outline:

1. Using Figure 2-13 as a guide, change the text of slides 2 and 3 of Carl's presentation by dragging I to select the text and then delete or retype it.

Figure 2-13 ◀
Text of slides
2 and 3

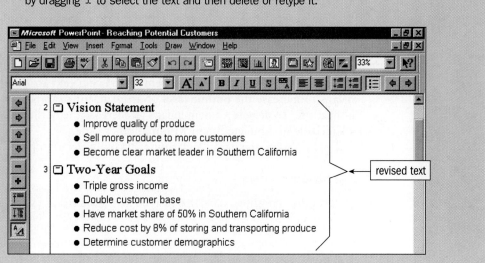

Your presentation window should now look like Figure 2-13.

Moving Text Up and Down in Outline View

As Carl reads through the text of the first three slides, he decides to switch the second and third items under "Two-Year Goals." Let's reverse the order of these items now.

To move an item of text in Outline View:

1. Click ✛ on the bullet to the left of the text "Have market share of 50% in Southern California." PowerPoint highlights the text.

2. Click the **Move Up** button ⬆ on the Outlining toolbar. PowerPoint moves the highlighted item up one position in the list, so the second and third items are switched. See Figure 2-14.

Figure 2-14 ◀
Moved
bulleted item

move Up button

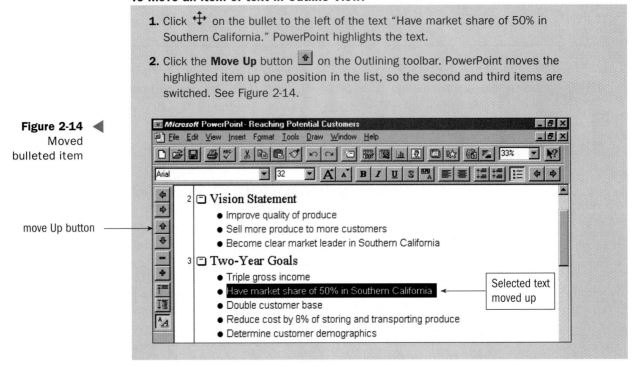

Selected text
moved up

You can use this same method to move entire slides. To move a slide, click ✛ on the slide icon of the slide you want to move, then click the Move Up button ⬆ or the Move Down button ⬇ on the Outlining toolbar to move the entire slide.

Promoting and Demoting the Outline Text

While reviewing the text of slide 3, Carl realizes that he needs to present more information on his customer demographics study. Rather than having "Determine customer demographics" as the last item of the main text of slide 3, Carl wants that phrase to be a title of a separate slide. Instead of deleting the bulleted item and then retyping it as a new slide title, you will promote the item from main text to slide title. To **promote** an item means to increase the outline level of an item, for example, to change a bulleted item to a slide title. To **demote** an item means to decrease the outline level, for example, to change a slide title to a bulleted item within another slide.

Let's promote the item "Determine customer demographics" to create the new slide.

To promote an item:

1. Click ⌶ anywhere within the bulleted item "Determine customer demographics" in slide 3.

2. Click the **Promote (Indent less)** button ⬅. This button is located in two places: on the Outlining toolbar and on the Formatting toolbar. When you click the Promote button, the text moves left and increases in size, and the new slide icon appears to the left of the text. The new slide becomes slide 4, and "Today's Situation" becomes slide 5, as shown in Figure 2-15.

Figure 2-15 ◀
Outline after
promoting text

promote button ⟶

demote button ⟶

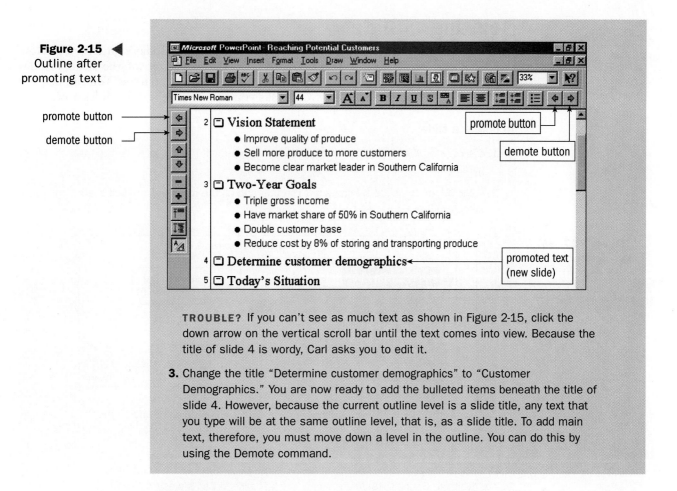

TROUBLE? If you can't see as much text as shown in Figure 2-15, click the down arrow on the vertical scroll bar until the text comes into view. Because the title of slide 4 is wordy, Carl asks you to edit it.

3. Change the title "Determine customer demographics" to "Customer Demographics." You are now ready to add the bulleted items beneath the title of slide 4. However, because the current outline level is a slide title, any text that you type will be at the same outline level, that is, as a slide title. To add main text, therefore, you must move down a level in the outline. You can do this by using the Demote command.

To demote an item:

1. Click I at the end of the title "Customer Demographics," then press the **Enter** key. PowerPoint creates a new slide 5.

2. Click the **Demote (Indent more)** button ⬕ on the Outlining or Formatting toolbar to change the outline level from slide title to main text and to indent. PowerPoint creates a bullet, and the insertion point appears to show that you are ready to enter text.

3. Type the main text of slide 4, as shown in Figure 2-16. Carefully check to make sure you have typed the information correctly. Make any necessary corrections.

Figure 2-16 ◀
Outline after
inserting text

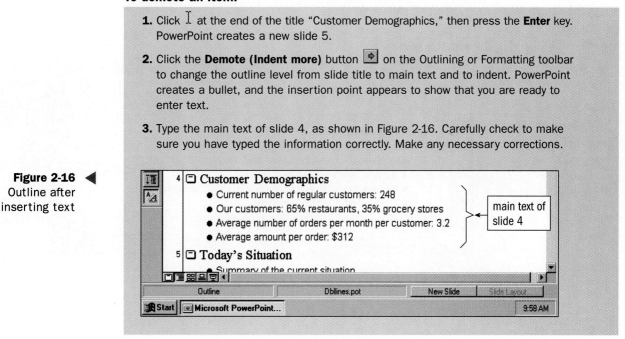

You have now created a new fourth slide for Carl's presentation.

Deleting a Slide

Carl feels that in his presentation he doesn't need slides on "Today's Situation," "How Did We Get Here?" or "Available Options," which are three of the default slides PowerPoint creates for you in the "Recommending a Strategy" outline. You can delete a slide in any view except Slide Show. Carl asks you to delete these three slides now.

To delete a slide:

1. Click ▼ on the vertical scroll bar until you can see all the text of slide 5 on the screen.

2. Click ✛ on the slide 5 slide icon. The title and all the main text of slide 5 are selected. See Figure 2-17.

Figure 2-17 ◀
Selected text to be deleted

selected slide icon ──────

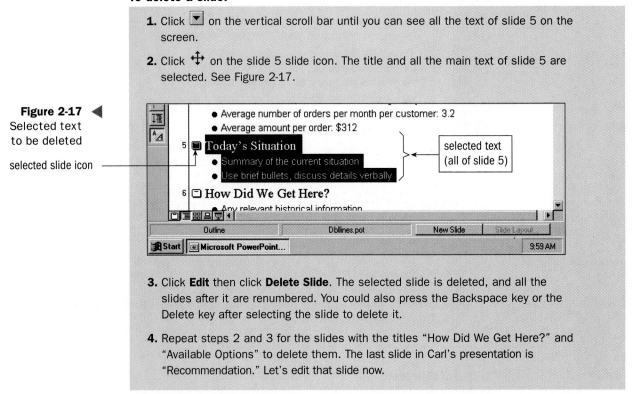

3. Click **Edit** then click **Delete Slide**. The selected slide is deleted, and all the slides after it are renumbered. You could also press the Backspace key or the Delete key after selecting the slide to delete it.

4. Repeat steps 2 and 3 for the slides with the titles "How Did We Get Here?" and "Available Options" to delete them. The last slide in Carl's presentation is "Recommendation." Let's edit that slide now.

To edit the last slide:

1. Edit the title of slide 5 to change "Recommendation" to "Recommendations."

2. Edit the main text of slide 5 so that the bulleted items match those in Figure 2-18.

Figure 2-18 ◀
Text of slide 5

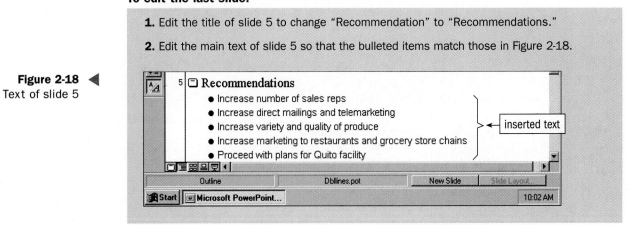

You have adapted and edited Carl's presentation in Outline View and completed the five slides of his presentation. He decides to use Slide View to see how his presentation looks.

Viewing Slides in Slide View

Viewing your presentation in Outline View doesn't show you how each of your slides will look when you actually make your presentation. To see the slides, you must change to one of the other views. Let's view the slides in Slide View.

To see slides in Slide View:

1. Scroll the presentation window so you can see the beginning of the outline, then click the pointer anywhere within the text of slide 1. This makes slide 1 the current slide, so that when you switch to Slide View, slide 1 will appear on the screen first.

2. Click the **Slide View** button 🔲 on the View toolbar to display slide 1 in the presentation window. After looking over the slide, you will view the next slide.

3. Click the **Next Slide** button ⬇ at the bottom of the vertical scroll bar to display slide 2, "Vision Statement." After looking at slide 2, you can view slide 3.

4. Drag the scroll box down until the message by the scroll box says that you're on slide 3, as shown in Figure 2-19, then release the mouse button. Now you can use the Next Slide button or the scroll box to review slides 4 and 5.

Figure 2-19 ◄
Moving scroll
box to slide 3

current slide in
presentation window

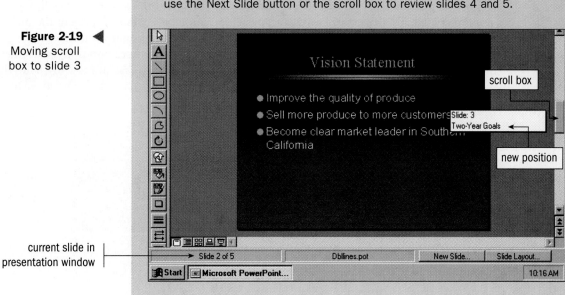

You can use Slide View to see what the slides will look like during Carl's presentation. This concludes Session 2.2. You can exit PowerPoint to return to the Windows 95 desktop or continue to the next session.

Quick Check

1. Explain how to do the following:
   a. Move text up in Outline View
   b. Delete a slide in Outline View
   c. Change placeholder text in Outline View
   d. Edit text in Outline View

2. What does it mean to promote a slide in Outline View?

3. What does it mean to demote a slide in Outline View?

4. Explain the benefits of Outline View over Slide View and the benefits of Slide View over Outline View.

SESSION
2.3

In this session you will learn how to edit text using cut-and-paste and drag-and-drop operations, as well as learn how to change the font, font size, and font color.
If you exited PowerPoint at the end of the previous session, start the program again, and open the presentation file "Reaching Potential Customers."

Moving Text Using Cut and Paste

Cut and paste is an important way to move text in PowerPoint. To **cut** means to remove text (or some other item) from the document and place it on the Windows clipboard. The **clipboard** is an area where text and graphics that have been cut or copied are stored until you act on them further. To **paste** means to transfer a copy of the text from the clipboard into the document. To perform a cut-and-paste operation, you simply highlight the material you want to move, cut it, and then paste the material where you want it.

As Carl reviews slide 3 ("Two-Year Goals") of his PowerPoint presentation, he decides that the text of the fourth bullet is awkward. He wants to move the phrase "by 8%" to the end of the fourth item, so that it becomes "Reduce cost of storing and transporting produce by 8%."

REFERENCE
window

CUTTING AND PASTING (MOVING) TEXT

- Select the text you want to move.
- Cut the selected text by clicking the Cut button on the Standard toolbar.
- Move the insertion point to the target location in the presentation.
- Paste the text back into the presentation by clicking the Paste button on the Standard toolbar.

Carl asks you to change the text using the cut-and-paste method.

To move text using cut and paste:

1. Make sure slide 3 appears in the PowerPoint window in Slide View. See Figure 2-20.

Figure 2-20 ◄
Slide 3
before revision

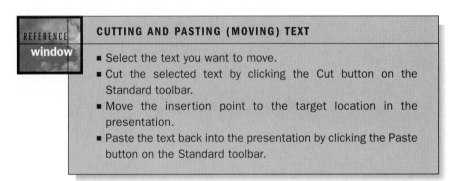

TROUBLE? If you don't see slide 3, use the Next Slide or Previous Slide buttons or the scroll box to move to slide 3.

2. Select the phrase "by 8%" in the fourth item of slide 3 by dragging I over it. See Figure 2-21.

Figure 2-21 ◀
Selected text
for cut and
paste

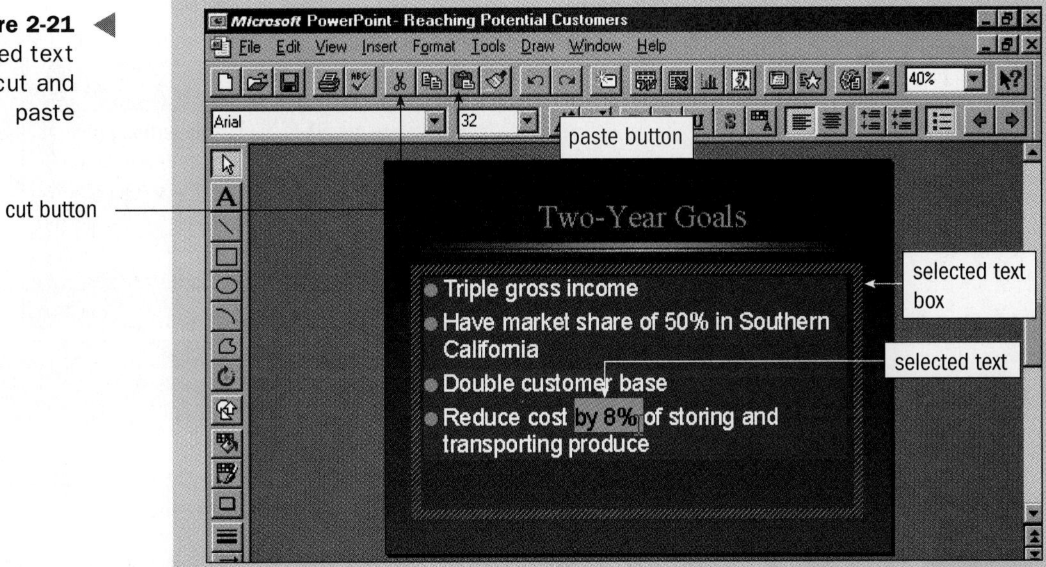

cut button ———

3. Click the **Cut** button 🔪 on the Standard toolbar. The phrase is deleted and automatically added to the clipboard.

4. Click I at the end of the phrase, "Reduce cost of storing and transporting produce." This puts the insertion point at the location where you want to paste the text back into the slide.

   TROUBLE? The insertion point may be hard to see with the PowerPoint default color scheme. If you can't see the insertion point, don't worry about it. Make sure you clicked I in the correct place, then go on to the next step.

5. Click the **Paste** button 📋 on the Standard toolbar. The phrase "by 8%" appears again in the slide, but this time at the end of the item. To copy selected text rather than move it, click the Copy button on the Standard toolbar instead of the Cut button. Then you can paste a copy of the text anywhere in the presentation.

Moving Text Using Drag and Drop

In addition to cut and paste, you can use **drag and drop** to move text in PowerPoint. You simply select the text by dragging the pointer over it, move the pointer into the selected area, press and hold down the left mouse button while you drag the text, and then release the mouse button when the selected text is positioned where you want it.

Carl wants you to move the words "of 50%" from the middle to the end of the sentence in the second bulleted item of slide 3. Let's move the phrase now.

To move text using drag and drop:

1. Select the phrase "of 50%."

2. Move the pointer within the region of the selected text, press and hold the mouse button, drag the pointer to the right of the word "California" in the same item of the main text, as shown in Figure 2-22, then release the mouse button. The phrase "of 50%" moves from the middle of the bulleted item to the end of the line.

Figure 2-22 ◀
Drag-and-drop
operation

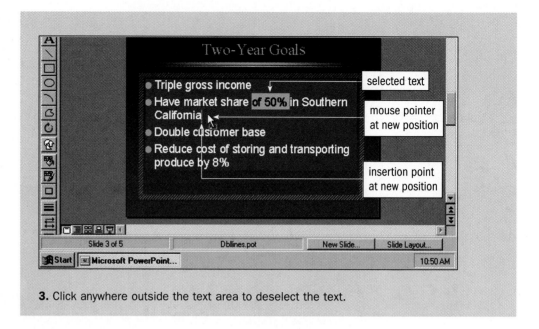

3. Click anywhere outside the text area to deselect the text.

Cut and paste and drag and drop are both effective in moving text from one location to another. You can use both methods in any view except Slide Show.

Adding a New Slide and Choosing a Layout

Carl created his presentation using the AutoContent Wizard, which gave him a ready-made outline to adapt to his own needs. However, you don't have to use a wizard to create a presentation. You can create it from scratch using the Blank Presentation option in the PowerPoint startup dialog box. PowerPoint displays blank slides to which you add your own text.

Carl decides his presentation needs a slide that summarizes Inca Import's new marketing plan, so he asks you to add a new slide. Let's add the slide in Slide View now.

To add a slide in Slide View:

1. With slide 3 still in the presentation window, click the **New Slide** button on the status bar. PowerPoint displays the New Slide dialog box. You could also click the **Insert New Slide** button on the Standard toolbar.

The New Slide dialog box appears on the screen. See Figure 2-23.

Figure 2-23 ◀
New Slide
dialog box

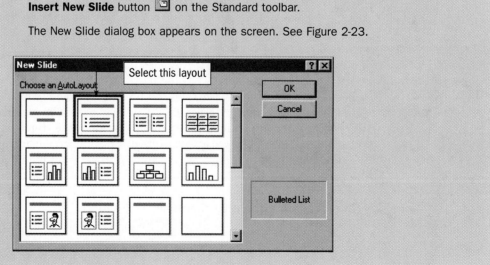

Before adding a new slide, you must decide where you want the placeholders for titles, text, and graphics to go. PowerPoint gives you the option of selecting from a variety of AutoLayout slides, which are preformatted slides with placeholders already added. You can also choose a blank layout.

2. Click on a few of the AutoLayouts and read their names in the lower-right corner of the dialog box. If you wanted to start with a blank slide, you would click the Blank layout, which is the fourth layout from the left on the third row. However, Carl wants his new slide to be a bulleted list.

3. If necessary, drag the scroll box on the AutoLayout scroll bar to the top of the scroll bar, then click the second layout in the top row, titled "Bulleted List." See Figure 2-23.

4. Click the **OK** button. PowerPoint inserts a new slide containing a title and main text placeholder for the bulleted list.

5. Click the **title placeholder** (where the slide says "Click to add title"), and type **Our New Marketing Campaign**.

6. Click the **main text placeholder**, then type the three bulleted items shown in Figure 2-24.

Figure 2-24
Completed
slide 4

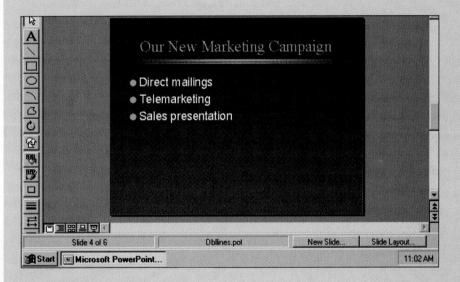

7. Click anywhere outside the text areas to deselect the text box. Slide 4 should now look like Figure 2-24.

You have now added a new slide, with a new layout.

Changing the Design Template

When you use the AutoContent Wizard or open a blank presentation, PowerPoint provides a predetermined **design template**, that is, the colors and format of the background and the type style of the titles, accents, and other text. The default design template that PowerPoint uses with the "Recommending a Strategy" option in the AutoContent Wizard is the Double Lines design template, in which double lines divide the title from the main text, the background is maroon, the title text is blue, and the main text is white. You can change the default design template to another one from among many more that PowerPoint provides. To change the design template, you click the Apply Design Template button on the Standard toolbar.

Carl wants you to change the template for his presentation. Let's change the template now.

To change the template:

1. Click the **Apply Design Template** button 🖵 on the Standard toolbar. The Apply Design Template dialog box appears. See Figure 2-25.

Figure 2-25 ◀
Apply Design
Template
dialog box

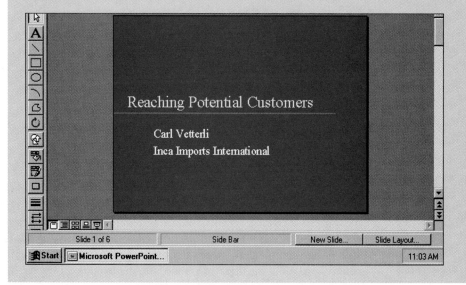

2. Scroll the design template names in the Name list box until you see **Side Bar**, then click that name. The selected design template appears in the preview box at the right of the dialog box.

   TROUBLE? If you don't have the Side Bar design template installed on your computer, choose any other template you like.

3. Click the **Apply** button to change the design template for all the slides in the presentation. The new design template will appear on all the slides in the presentation, and its name (Side Bar) is displayed on the status bar. Carl wants to see what the new design template looks like in the title slide.

4. Move to slide 1 by dragging the scroll box to the top of the vertical scroll bar. The title slide appears in the window. See Figure 2-26.

Figure 2-26 ◀
Title slide with
new design
template

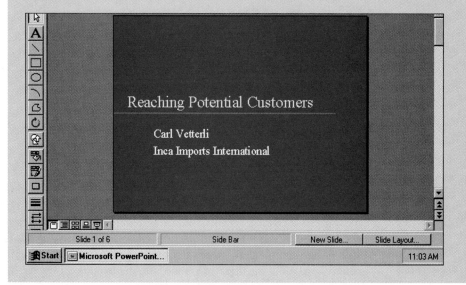

Carl likes the look of the title slide.

Formatting Text

When Carl created his presentation, he used PowerPoint's default fonts for his slide show. A **font** is a set of characters (letters, digits, and other characters such as !, @, and *) that have a certain design and appearance. Each font has a name, such as Courier, Times New Roman, or Arial (see Figure 2-27). The current font is listed on the left of the Formatting toolbar. The default font in the Side Bar design template is Times New Roman. (Your toolbar might indicate a different font, depending on your printer and on which fonts are installed on your system.) The height of a font is measured in points. A **point** is ½ of an inch.

Figure 2-27 ◀
Sample fonts

Font appearances are sometimes classified as serif or sans serif. See Figure 2-28. A **serif font** is a font that has small embellishments at the end of the line strokes on each character. Examples of serif fonts include Times New Roman, Courier, and Century Schoolbook. A **sans serif font** is a font that lacks the embellishments at the end of the line strokes on the characters. Examples of sans serif fonts include Arial, Helvetica, Avant Garde, and Humanist.

Figure 2-28 ◀
Serif and sans
serif fonts

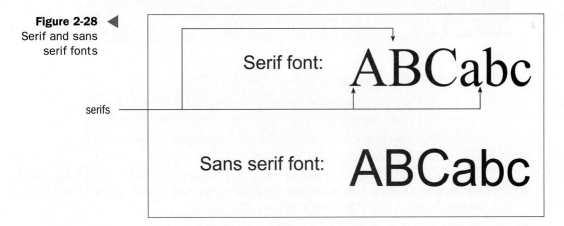

You can change the font, size, style (bold, italic, underlined), and color of text in PowerPoint. PowerPoint does a good job of selecting fonts for the slides; however, there may be times when you want to change PowerPoint's defaults.

TYPOGRAPHY GUIDELINES

- The size of the text should reflect the importance level of the text, that is, titles should be larger than main text.
- Use large fonts (24 through 60 points) for maximum readability.
- Vary type styles to provide emphasis, but remember that having too much emphasis is the same as having none.
- Words in all uppercase can decrease reading speed. It's easier to read words in mostly lowercase letters because the shapes of the letters help the reader see the words as a unit.

CHANGING THE FONT, FONT SIZE, AND FONT STYLE

- Select the text that you want to change.
- Click the appropriate button on the Formatting toolbar.

To change the font of selected text, click the Font down arrow and choose the desired font. To change the font size, click the Font Size down arrow and choose the desired size, or click the Increase/Decrease Font Size buttons. To change the font style, click the Bold, Italics, Underline, or Text Shadow buttons.

Carl now decides that the text for his name and the company's name on the title slide would look better in two different colors, rather than in the same text color.

PRINCIPLES OF USING COLOR ON A SLIDE

- Color can focus the reader's attention.
- Color can establish understanding through associations (for example, red as a warning).
- Color can reveal organization and pattern by using similar colors for related ideas.
- Too much color can be distracting and slow down reading and comprehension.

Carl wants you to change the color of the text "Inca Imports International" on slide 1. PowerPoint doesn't allow you to change the color of the text from Outline View, but you can change the color from Slide View.

CHANGING THE COLOR OF THE TEXT

- Make sure you are in Slide View.
- Select the text that you want to change.
- Click the Text Color button on the Formatting toolbar.
- Choose the desired color.

Let's change the color of the company's name.

To change the color of the text:

1. Click anywhere on the company's name, then drag I to select the phrase "Inca Imports International."

2. Click the **Text Color** button on the Formatting toolbar to display a small grid of colors. See Figure 2-29.

Figure 2-29 ◀
Changing
text color

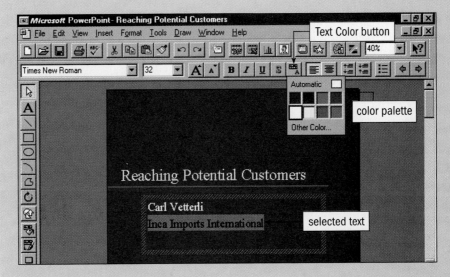

3. Click the **yellow tile** (small square) on the Text Color menu. The color of the company's name changes to yellow, although you can't see that color yet because the text is selected.

4. Deselect the text by clicking the pointer anywhere in the slide except on text. The title slide now looks like Figure 2-30.

Figure 2-30 ◀
Slide 1 after
changing
text color

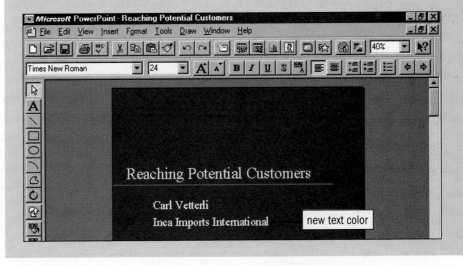

By making appropriate changes in the font style and color, you can improve the appearance and readability of the text of your slide show.

Saving the Final Version of the Presentation

Now that Carl's presentation is complete, you are ready to save the final version. Because you have saved the presentation previously, you can simply click the Save button to save the current version of the file over the now obsolete version.

To save a file that has been saved previously:

1. Make sure your Student Disk is in the disk drive.

2. Click the **Save** button 🖫 on the Standard toolbar to save the file using its current filename, "Reaching Potential Customers."

A copy of the updated presentation is now on your Student Disk.

Viewing the Completed Slide Show

Carl wants to see his completed slide show.

To view the completed presentation as a slide show:

1. Make sure you're viewing slide 1 in Slide View, so slide 1 will appear on the screen first.

2. Click the **Slide Show** button 🖳 on the View toolbar.

3. After you read a slide, click the left mouse button or press the **spacebar** to advance to the next slide. Continue advancing until you have seen the entire slide show and PowerPoint returns to Slide View or Outline View.

Previewing and Printing the Presentation

Carl wants you to print handouts for his presentation so he will have a hard copy for his records. Before printing on your black-and-white printer, you should preview the presentation to make sure the text is legible in black and white. Let's do that now.

To preview print handouts of the presentation:

1. Make sure you're in Slide View, then click the **B&W View** button 🖾 on the Standard toolbar, and make sure slide 1 appears on the screen. See Figure 2-31.

Figure 2-31 ◀
Slide in Black–
and–White
View

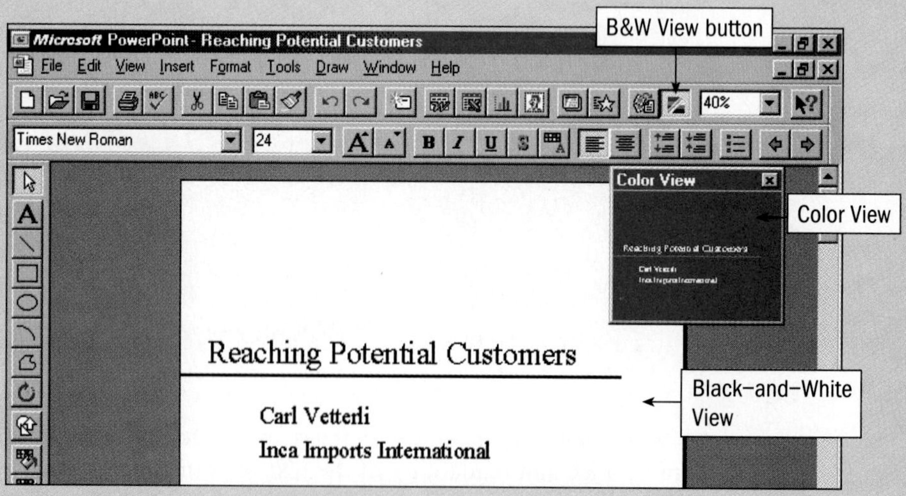

2. Look at the text on each slide to make sure it is readable. Everything looks fine, so you can click the **B&W View** button 🖾 again to return to color view.

3. Click **File** then click **Print** button to open the Print dialog box. Don't click the Print button on the Standard toolbar or PowerPoint will immediately start printing without letting you change the print settings.

4. Click the Print what list arrow, and select **Handouts (2 slides per page)**.

5. If you're using a black-and-white printer, make sure the **Black & White** check box on the Print dialog box is selected. See Figure 2-32.

Figure 2-32 ◄
Print
dialog box

select 2 slides
per page

select this

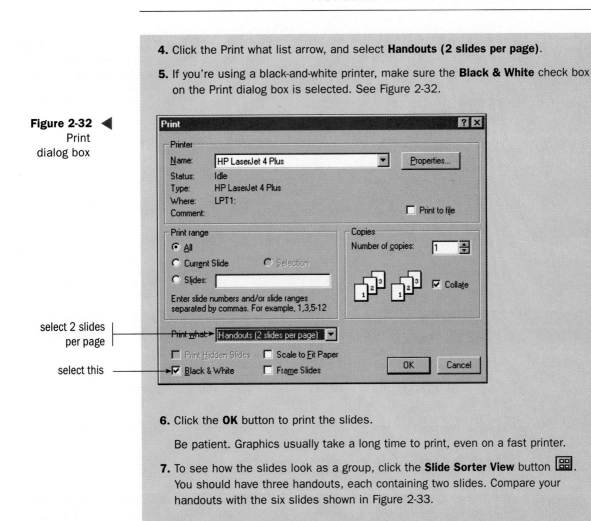

6. Click the **OK** button to print the slides.

Be patient. Graphics usually take a long time to print, even on a fast printer.

7. To see how the slides look as a group, click the **Slide Sorter View** button 🔳. You should have three handouts, each containing two slides. Compare your handouts with the six slides shown in Figure 2-33.

Figure 2-33 ◄
Completed
slide
presentation in
Slide Sorter
View

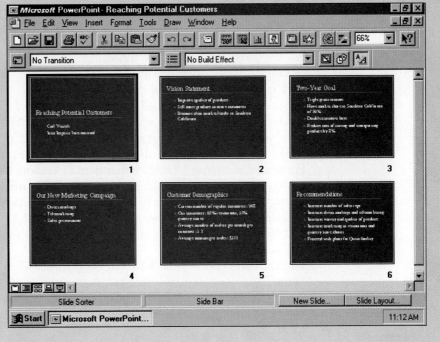

Carl now has a hard copy of his presentation.

Now that you have created, edited, saved, and printed Carl's presentation, you can exit PowerPoint. If PowerPoint asks if you want to save changes to the presentation file, click the Yes button. Your computer screen now displays the Windows 95 desktop.

Quick Check

1. Explain how to do the following:
   a. Change the color of a font
   b. Increase the size of a font
   c. Add a slide in Slide View
   d. Move text using cut and paste in any view
   e. Move text using drag and drop in any view

2. What is a design template?

3. Define or describe the following terms:
   a. font
   b. points
   c. serif font
   d. sans serif font

4. After you've made an editing change in PowerPoint, how do you undo it?

5. Give one advantage and one disadvantage of a cut-and-paste operation versus a drag-and-drop operation.

6. How do you change the presentation design template?

Tutorial Assignments

In the following Tutorial Assignments, make sure you click the Open an Existing File button when you start PowerPoint (or the Open button on the Standard toolbar) and then open each file. After working with a presentation and saving your changes, close the presentation.

Open the file Campaign from the TAssign folder on your Student Disk, save the file as New Marketing Campaign, and do the following:

1. In Outline View, delete the unnecessary articles "a," "an," and "the" from each main text slide.
2. In Slide View, change the color of the title of slide 1 from white to red.
3. In Outline View, move the second item in slide 3, "Will develop slide presentation," down so that it becomes the third (last) item in the main text.
4. In slide 4, the third item of the main text is "Step #2. Establishing Contact with Potential Customers." Promote that item to become a slide title (new slide 5).
5. In the new slide 6, demote the second, third, and fourth bulleted items so that they appear indented beneath the first item, "Organize data for our market advantage".
6. In slides 4 through 7, change the phrases "Step #1," "Step #2," "Step #3," and "Step #4" (but not the text that follows these phrases in the slide titles) to any sans serif font.
7. Edit the main text of slide 8 so that the phrase "Must hire" becomes simply "Hire."
8. In slide 2, move (using cut and paste or drag and drop) the phrase "by telephone" so it immediately follows the phrase "Follow up" in the same item of the main text.
9. Move the entire slide 9 ("Key Issues") up to become slide 8, so that "Becoming More Effective" is the last slide.
10. In slide 2, underline the phrase "New Marketing Campaign."

11. Check the spelling within the presentation by using the Spelling button on the Standard toolbar or by clicking Tools, then clicking Spelling. When PowerPoint stops at a word that is misspelled, click the correctly spelled word from within the Suggestions, so that it becomes the "Change To" word, and then click the Change button. If PowerPoint stops at a word that is actually spelled correctly but that it doesn't recognize, click the Ignore button.

12. View the entire presentation in Slide Show View.

13. Use the Save command to save the presentation to your Student Disk using the default filename.

14. Print the outline of the presentation.

15. Close the file.

Open the file Restruct, save the file as Proposed Restructuring, and do the following:

16. Change the design template. Choose the design template you think looks best.

17. In slide 1, change the text of the name of the author ("Angelena Cristenas") to another color.

18. In the title of slide 2, change "Goal and Objective" to "Objectives."

19. In slide 5, change the title to "Restructuring is Best."

20. Also in slide 5, change the size of the font in the title from 44 to 60 points.

21. Insert a new slide between slides 1 and 2 by doing the following: Move the insertion point anywhere within the text of slide 1 in Outline View, then click the Insert New Slide button on the Standard toolbar. (You can also click Insert, then click New Slide.)

22. With the insertion point to the right of the slide icon for the new slide 2, type the title, "Vision Statement."

23. For the main text in the new slide 2, type the text of the first bulleted item: "Inca Imports can become the premier produce import company in Southern California." Then type the text of the second bulleted item: "Inca Imports can triple sales in the next two years."

24. In the new slide 2, change the color of the words "premier" and "triple" to another color.

25. Edit the main text you added to slide 2 to follow the 6 × 6 rule as closely as possible.

26. Check the spelling within the presentation by using the Spelling button on the Standard toolbar or by clicking Tools, then clicking Spelling. When PowerPoint stops at a word that is misspelled, click the correctly spelled word from within the Suggestions, so that it becomes the "Change To" word, and then click the Change button. If PowerPoint stops at a word that is actually spelled correctly but that it doesn't recognize, click the Ignore button.

27. View the entire presentation in Slide Show View.

28. Use the Save button to save the presentation to your Student Disk using the default filename.

29. Preview the slides in Black-and-White View. If any text is unreadable, change the design template to one that is readable in black and white.

30. Print a copy of the outline of the presentation.

31. Save using the default filename and close the file.

Case Problems

1. New Weave Fashions Shaunda Shao works for New Weave Fashions, a clothing supplier for specialty retail stores in the Northwest. New Weave contracts with wholesale fashion centers to supply New Weave retailers with women's shoes, sports fashions, and boutique merchandise. Shaunda's job is to provide training for New Weave's fledgling retailers.

Open the file Newweave from the Cases folder on your Student Disk, save the file as Case 1-New Weave, and do the following:

1. Increase the font size of the title of slide 1 from 44 to 60 points.
2. In the first bulleted item in slide 2, use cut and paste to move the year ("1997") from the end of the line of text to the beginning, delete the word "in" that now appears at the end of the line, and change "Sales" to "sales."
3. In the second bulleted item in slide 2, use drag and drop to move "increased only 5.5%" from the middle of the line to the end of the line of text.
4. In slide 4, divide the second item into two separate items, and then revise the results so that they become "Obtaining volume discounts," and "Obtaining quick, reliable delivery."
5. Also in slide 4, move the last item ("Competing with well-known stores") so it becomes the second item in the main text of slide 2.
6. In slide 6, promote the phrase "Telephone follow-ups" so that it is on the same level as the bulleted item above it.

7. Change the color of the title of slide 1 to yellow. *Hint*: When you click the Text Color button on the Formatting toolbar, yellow might not appear there, so click Other color, then click one of the yellow tiles.
8. Check the spelling within the presentation by using the Spelling button on the Standard toolbar or by clicking Tools, then clicking Spelling. When PowerPoint stops at a word that is misspelled, click the correctly spelled word from within the Suggestions, so that it becomes the "Change To" word, and then click the Change button. If PowerPoint stops at a word that is actually spelled correctly but that it doesn't recognize, click the Ignore button.
9. Use Slide Show to view all the slides of the presentation.
10. Preview the slides in Black-and-White View. If some of the text is illegible, change the design template to make the text readable.
11. Save the file using its default filename.
12. Print the outline of the presentation.
13. Print the slides (as two slides per page) in black and white.
14. Close the file.

2. InfoTech Pratt Deitschmann is seeking venture capital in the amount of $2.5 million for his startup company, InfoTech. InfoTech provides mailroom, word processing, in-house printing, and other information-output services for large corporations and law practices. Pratt has created a presentation to give to executives at A.B. O'Dair & Company, a New York City investment banking firm.

Open the file Infotech, save the file as Case 2 - InfoTech, and do the following:

1. Change the font of the title of slide 1 to a sans serif font, such as Arial or Futura.
2. Change the size of the title from 44 to 54 points.
3. Delete "and Objective" from the title of slide 2.
4. Delete the first item of the main text of slide 4.
5. In slide 4, promote the four items that are double-indented to single-indented, so that all items in the main text are at the same level.
6. In slide 4, change the color of the phrase "5% lower" to yellow.
7. In slide 5, move the second item of the main text to become the third (last) item.
8. Move slide 5 so it becomes slide 6.
9. In slide 7, use drag and drop to move the text and make other changes so that the first item becomes "Initial venture capital of $2.5 million."
10. Use Slide Show View to view the entire presentation.
11. Save the file using the current filename.
12. Preview the slides in black and white to make sure they are all readable. If any text isn't readable, change the design template to one that makes all text readable.
13. Print the slides (as two slides per page) and the outline of the presentation.
14. Close the file.

3. Team One Facilities Management Virgil Pino works for Team One Facilities Management, an international company that manages municipal waste disposal facilities. Virgil must communicate the unfortunate news that escalating travel costs threaten Team One's profitability. Do the following:

1. Close any presentation that might be in the PowerPoint presentation window.
2. Begin a new presentation by clicking File, then clicking New on the menu bar. In the New Presentation dialog box, click the Presentation Designs tab and click the International icon, then click the OK button.
3. In the New Slide dialog, click the Title Slide AutoLayout button and click the OK button.
4. In Slide View replace the slide placeholders with the presentation title, "Rescuing Our Road Warriors," and the name of the author, "Virgil Pino."

5. Virgil has already created some of the text for other slides, so insert the file "Teamone" into the current presentation. *Hint*: Click Insert, click Slides from File, and select "Teamone" from the Student Disk.
6. With slide 2, "Our Situation," in the presentation window in Slide View, change the word "profitability" in the last bulleted item from white to yellow.
7. In slide 3, add a new bulleted item between the last and the next-to-the-last items. Type the text of the item, "Cost per trip increased by 30%."

8. Insert a new slide 4, and from the New Slide dialog box, choose the AutoLayout named "Bulleted list," located on the first row, second column of the AutoLayout box, then click the OK button. Make the title of the slide "Alternatives Considered." Type the following four items in the main text of the slide:
   a. Decrease amount of travel
   b. Decrease travel costs
   c. Increase other means of networking
   d. Increase efficiency of each trip
9. In slide 5, delete the item, "Coordinate trips to visit more clients per trip."
10. Switch to Outline View, and promote the item "Managers' Vision for the Future" so that it becomes the title of a new slide (slide 6).
11. In slide 6, move the first item in the main text so it becomes the last item.
12. In Outline View, add a new slide 7, with the title "Summary" and with the bulleted items "Change to meet growth," "Overcome efficiency gap," "Manage travel time and money better," and "Rescue our road warriors."

13. Create a new slide 8 while still in Outline View. Then go into Slide View and change the Slide Layout to "Blank." *Hint*: To change a slide layout, click Format, click Slide Layout, select the Blank layout slide, then click the Apply button.
14. Save the presentation using the filename Rescuing Our Road Warriors.
15. Preview the slides in black and white, then print them (two slides per page).
16. Close the file.

4. Presentation on Selling an Idea The chair of your college department has asked you to participate in an orientation for high school students who are considering attending your college and majoring in your subject area. The chair has asked you to prepare and give a 20-minute presentation on the advantages of majoring in your specialty. In other words, you need to "sell" your major to the incoming students. Prepare an on-screen presentation with the following features:

1. Use the AutoContent Wizard to begin developing an outline on "Selling a Product, Service, or Idea." *Hint*: To start the AutoContent Wizard while PowerPoint is already running, click File, then click New. (Don't use the New button on the Standard toolbar.) On the New Presentation dialog box, click the Presentations tab, then double-click the AutoContent Wizard icon.
2. Enter your name and other personal information when prompted to do so.
3. Make the title of your presentation (that is, what you're going to talk about) "Majoring in..." (with the name of your major). If you haven't selected a major, use one that you're considering.

4. Change the design template to Color Boxes, or to another template of your choice if Color Boxes is not available on your system.
5. In slide 1, change the color of the title from white to lime green.
6. Switch to Outline View.
7. In slide 2, change the main text placeholders to objectives of your presentation. For example, you might want to use bulleted items such as "To show that... is a good major," "To give overview of requirements," and "To list future jobs for... majors." Include at least three objectives.
8. In slide 3, change "Customer Requirements" to "What You Want in a Major," then list three to six items that constitute a good major, such as "Challenging," "Satisfying," "Job Opportunities," and "Job Flexibility."
9. In slide 4, change "Meeting the Needs" to "Meeting Your Needs," then list in the main text several ways in which your major meets students' needs.
10. Delete slide 5, "Cost Analysis."
11. In the new slide 5, "Our Strengths," list some strengths of your department, such as "Friendly faculty," "Moderate course load," and "Opportunities for research."
12. In slide 6, "Key Benefits," list the benefits of your major.
13. Delete slide 7.
14. Add a new slide 7, "Summary," in which you summarize key points of your presentation.
15. Preview the presentation in Slide Show View and Black-and-White View.
16. Save the presentation as Majoring in... (with the name of your major).
17. Print the outline of your presentation.
18. Close the file.

Creating Graphics for Your Slides

Creating a Sales Presentation for Inca Imports

OBJECTIVES

In this tutorial you will:

- Resize and move text boxes and graphics boxes

- Change the general layout of an existing slide

- Insert pictures and clip-art images

- Create graphs and organization charts

- Draw and manipulate graphic shapes

CASE

Inca Sales Presentation

Using the information gathered previously on customers of Inca Imports International, Enrique Hoffmann, Director of Marketing, and his staff have identified other businesses in the Southern California area that fit the profile of potential new customers. Enrique and his staff will focus their marketing efforts at these retail customers, who would benefit from having a wide range of fresh produce, year-round availability, and good customer service. Enrique and his staff are ready to prepare a presentation for these prospective clients.

In this tutorial you will revise Enrique's current version of the presentation by reformatting and adding graphics to some of the slides. A **graphic** is a picture, clip art, graph, chart, or table that you can add to a slide.

SESSION

3.1

In this session you'll learn how to resize and move text boxes, how to insert pictures and clip-art images, and how to move and resize graphics boxes.

USING GRAPHICS EFFECTIVELY

You should use graphics in the following situations:
- To present information that words can't communicate effectively
- To interest and motivate the reader
- To communicate relationships quickly
- To increase understanding and retention

Planning the Presentation

The marketing staff begins by planning their presentation:

- **Purpose of the presentation:** To convince business owners who do not now buy from Inca Imports to start buying our products and services

- **Type of presentation:** A 45-minute sales presentation

  Audience: Retail buyers and other business representatives

- **Location of presentation:** A conference room at the offices of Inca Imports

- **Audience needs:** To recognize their need for Inca's products and services and to understand how Inca Imports differs from other produce suppliers

- **Format:** One speaker presenting an electronic slide show consisting of five to seven slides

Manually Changing the Text Layout

After planning the presentation, Enrique and his staff created slides containing only text, knowing that they would need to add graphics to make the presentation more interesting and effective. Enrique has asked you to make the changes. Let's first start PowerPoint and open the current draft of Enrique's presentation.

To open an existing presentation and save it with a new name:

1. Start PowerPoint and, if necessary, close the Tip of the Day dialog box. The PowerPoint startup dialog box appears on the screen. You will now retrieve the presentation that Enrique created using the AutoContent Wizard.

2. Make sure the PowerPoint Student Disk is in the disk drive, then click the **Open Existing Presentation** button in the PowerPoint startup dialog box, and click the **OK** button or press the **Enter** key. The Open dialog box appears on the screen.

   TROUBLE? If the PowerPoint startup dialog box does not appear on your screen, click the Open button on the Standard toolbar to display the Open dialog box.

3. Open the **Tutorial.03** folder on your Student Disk.

4. Click **Incasale** in the Names list box, then click the **Open** button. The file "Incasale" appears in the presentation window. See Figure 3-1.

Figure 3-1
Presentation
window in
Outline View
with outline of
Inca Sales
Presentation

selected slide —

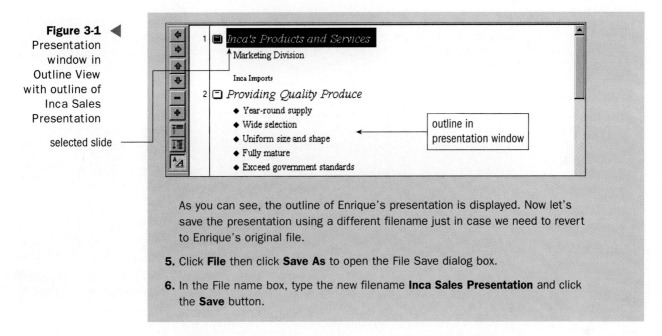

As you can see, the outline of Enrique's presentation is displayed. Now let's save the presentation using a different filename just in case we need to revert to Enrique's original file.

5. Click **File** then click **Save As** to open the File Save dialog box.

6. In the File name box, type the new filename **Inca Sales Presentation** and click the **Save** button.

Enrique is satisfied with his outline, and now he wants you to add graphics to the slide. To do this, you will work in Slide View, which allows you to view and modify the position, size, and alignment of text boxes and graphics. **Text boxes** are the regions of the slide that contain text. On the title slide (slide 1) of Enrique's presentation, there are two text boxes: the first text box contains the presentation title ("Inca's Products and Services"), and the second text box contains the subtitle ("Marketing Division" with the company's name "Inca Imports"). Text boxes and graphics are objects. An **object** is any item (text box, clip art, graph, organization chart, or picture) on a slide that you can move, resize, rotate, or otherwise manipulate.

On the title slide, Enrique wants you to change the location of the text boxes for the title and subtitle and then add the company's logo. A company logo is a visual identification for the company. You will need to make room for the logo by moving the two text boxes on the slide.

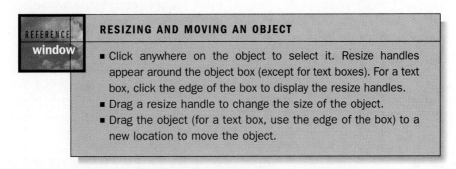

REFERENCE window

RESIZING AND MOVING AN OBJECT

■ Click anywhere on the object to select it. Resize handles appear around the object box (except for text boxes). For a text box, click the edge of the box to display the resize handles.
■ Drag a resize handle to change the size of the object.
■ Drag the object (for a text box, use the edge of the box) to a new location to move the object.

Let's rearrange the text boxes to fit the logo on the left side of the slide.

To resize and move text on a slide:

1. Make sure slide 1, "Inca's Products and Services," is selected (or the insertion point is somewhere within the text of slide 1) in Outline View, then click the **Slide View** button ☐ on the View toolbar. PowerPoint switches from Outline View to Slide View. Now you're ready to select and rearrange the text boxes.

2. If the presentation window isn't maximized, click the **Maximize** button ☐ in the upper-right corner of the presentation window. You should be able to see the entire slide.

3. Click I anywhere in the text of the title "Inca's Products and Services." The text box appears. See Figure 3-2. Notice that the text is aligned along the left edge of the text box.

Figure 3-2 ◀
Presentation window after selecting an object

selected text box ──

insertion point (can be anywhere in text) ──

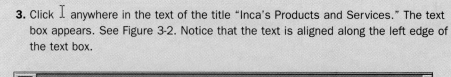

4. Click anywhere on the edge of the text box to display the resize handles around the text box. See Figure 3-3. **Resize handles** are small squares in the corners and on the edges of a text box or graphics box, which, when dragged with the pointer, change the size of the box.

Figure 3-3 ◀
Selected text box with resize handles

resize handle ──

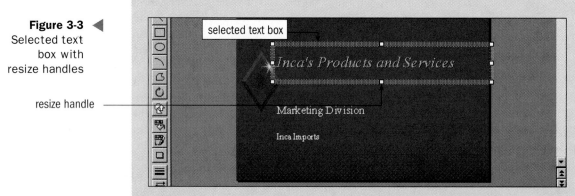

TROUBLE? If, when you try to click the edge, the text box becomes deselected, click the text again, then click exactly on the box edge.

5. Position the pointer over the resize handle in the lower-left corner of the text box.

6. Press and hold the mouse button, then drag the resize handle down and to the right to make the text box the approximate dimensions shown in Figure 3-4. Notice that a dotted outline of the text box follows the pointer movements. Don't worry about making the text box the exact size, in the same location shown in the figure. Just resize it as closely as you can.

Figure 3-4 ◀
Resizing the text box

pointer ──

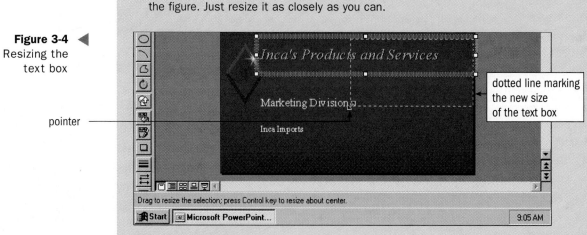

7. Release the mouse button. The text is now on two lines instead of one line.

8. Position the pointer on the right center resize handle of the title text box, and drag the resize handle to the left. See Figure 3-5.

Figure 3-5 ◀
Resizing the
text box

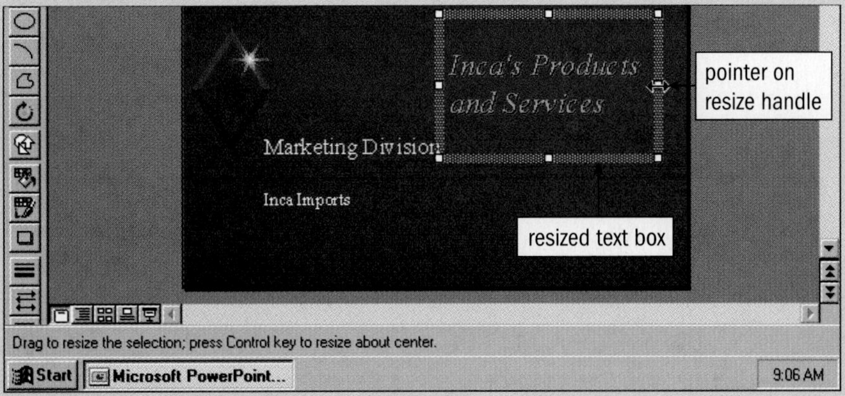

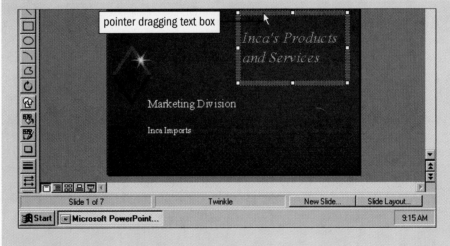

The title text box is the desired size and shape, but you will need to move it up so that it isn't so close to the subtitle. Let's move the box up now.

To move a selected object:

1. Make sure the title text box is selected, with the resize handles showing.

2. Click the outline of the text box and drag the edge of the selected text box up, until it is in the position shown in Figure 3-6.

Figure 3-6 ◀
Text box after
moving it up

TROUBLE? If the size of the text box increases as you move it up, then you selected a handle instead of the outline of the text box. Click Edit, then click Undo Resize Move and repeat Steps 1 and 2.

Enrique now wants to align the two text boxes along their left margins. Let's do that now.

To align and move the text boxes:

1. With the "Inca's Products" text box still selected, press and hold down the **Shift** key, click the text box with the subtitle "Marketing Division," then release the **Shift** key. Now both the title box and the subtitle box are selected. As you can see, by holding down the Shift key while you click text on a slide, you can select

more than one text box at a time. Notice that only the resize handles of the two text boxes are visible, not the box outlines. You can modify all of the selected text at once. Next we will align the left edges of the two text boxes and then move the text boxes to the right.

2. Click **Draw**, click **Align**, and then click **Lefts**. The text boxes are aligned along their left edges.

3. With the two text boxes still selected, position the pointer ⌖ in one of the text boxes, then drag the boxes to the right as far as they will go.

TROUBLE? If the text box resize handles disappeared when you clicked the mouse button, you clicked outside the text boxes. Select the text boxes again, then repeat Step 3.

4. Click anywhere outside the text to deselect the two text boxes. Your slide should now look like Figure 3-7.

Figure 3-7 ◀
Slide after
resizing and
repositioning
text boxes

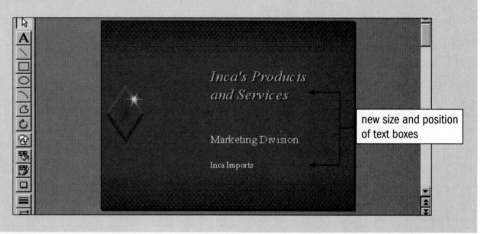

new size and position
of text boxes

Enrique wants you to insert the company's logo to the left of the text boxes that you just resized and moved, but the twinkling diamond-shaped graphic is in the way. Your next task is to remove the graphic from this slide only.

Removing a Background Graphic from a Slide

Enrique's slide presentation uses the design template called "Twinkle" because it has a twinkling diamond-shaped graphic, called a background graphic. A **background graphic** is a graphic located on a title master or slide master slide that appears in the background of all the slides in the presentation. You can, however, remove a background graphic from any one or all of the slides in your presentation. Let's remove the background graphic from the title slide.

To remove a background graphic:

1. With slide 1 still in the presentation window in Slide View, click **Format**, then click **Custom Background**. The Custom Background dialog box opens. See Figure 3-8.

Figure 3-8 ◀
Custom
Background
dialog box

click here to remove
background graphics

2. Click the **Omit Background Graphics from Master** check box to select it. This tells PowerPoint that you don't want the background graphic on the selected slide.

3. Click the **Apply** button (*not* the Apply to All button).

   TROUBLE? If you accidentally clicked the Apply to All button, PowerPoint removed the background graphic from all of the slides. You'll have to restore it to all of the slides by clicking Edit, then clicking Undo. Then repeat the steps.

Now that you have changed the size, position, and alignment of the text boxes and removed the background graphic from the title slide, you are ready to insert the company's logo in the slide.

Inserting a Picture into a Slide

Enrique now wants you to insert the Inca Imports International logo, a computer-generated image of fruit, to the left of the text boxes.

REFERENCE window	**INSERTING A PICTURE INTO A SLIDE**
	■ Click Insert, then click Picture to display the Picture dialog box. ■ Select the desired picture file from the disk, then click the OK button. ■ Move and resize the picture as desired.

Let's insert the logo now.

To insert a picture into a slide:

1. With slide 1 showing in Slide View, click **Insert**, then click **Picture**. The Insert Picture dialog box opens on the screen.

2. Open the **Tutorial.03** folder on your Student Disk.

3. Click **Incalogo** in the File name list to select the Inca Imports International logo, then click the **OK** button. The picture appears in the middle of the slide. The picture remains selected, as you can see from the handles around the edge of the graphic.

4. With the logo still selected, drag the graphics box to the left of the text so that the top edge of the logo is aligned with the top of the title text. See Figure 3-9. Click anywhere outside the slide to deselect the picture.

Figure 3-9 ◀
Slide after
inserting
picture

Inca logo ——

resize handles ——

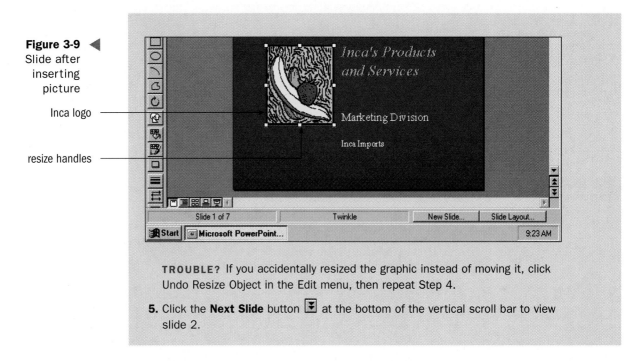

TROUBLE? If you accidentally resized the graphic instead of moving it, click Undo Resize Object in the Edit menu, then repeat Step 4.

5. Click the **Next Slide** button ⬇ at the bottom of the vertical scroll bar to view slide 2.

You have completed editing slide 1 and are ready to work on slide 2 of Enrique's presentation.

Changing the Slide Layout

Enrique wants you to add an item to the bulleted list in slide 2, "Providing Quality Produce." He decides that with the addition of this item, the bulleted list will be too long to fit on the slide. The slide might look better with two columns. To make the change, you could reformat the slide manually, but you decide to use the Slide Layout feature of PowerPoint. A **Slide Layout** is a predefined arrangement of placeholders on the slide for inserting the slide title, text, or graphics.

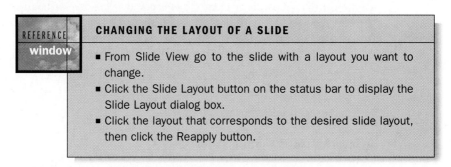

REFERENCE
window

CHANGING THE LAYOUT OF A SLIDE

- From Slide View go to the slide with a layout you want to change.
- Click the Slide Layout button on the status bar to display the Slide Layout dialog box.
- Click the layout that corresponds to the desired slide layout, then click the Reapply button.

Let's change the layout of slide 2 now to accommodate a second column of text.

To change the layout of an existing slide:

1. Click the **Slide Layout** button on the status bar. PowerPoint displays the Slide Layout dialog box. See Figure 3-10.

Figure 3-10 ◀
Slide Layout
dialog box

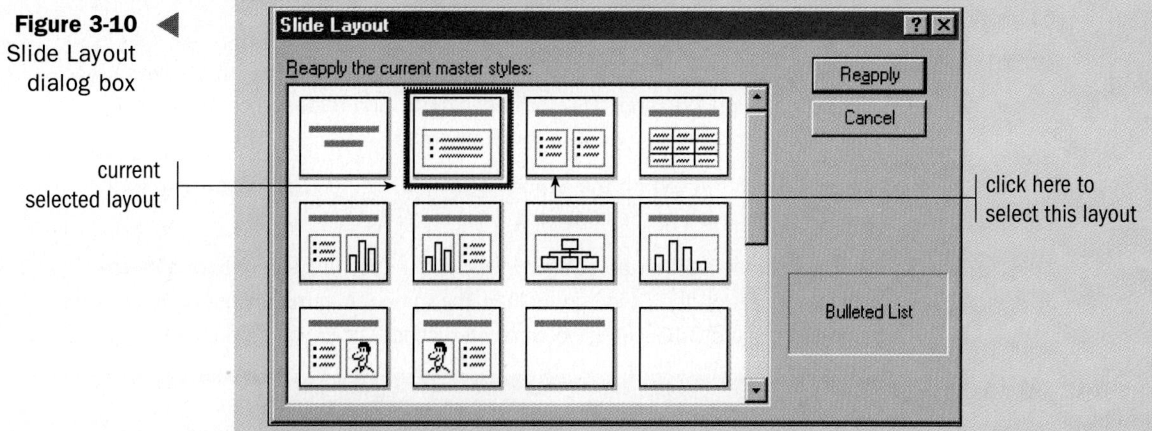

current
selected layout

click here to
select this layout

2. Click the layout called **2 Column Text**.

TROUBLE? If you're not sure which is the 2 Column Text layout, click each picture until the box at the lower right of the dialog box displays the name "2 Column Text." On most computers, it is the picture in the first row, third column, as shown in Figure 3-10.

3. Click the **Apply** button. PowerPoint reformats the slide, with a new text box placeholder on the right. See Figure 3-11.

Figure 3-11 ◀
Slide with
new layout

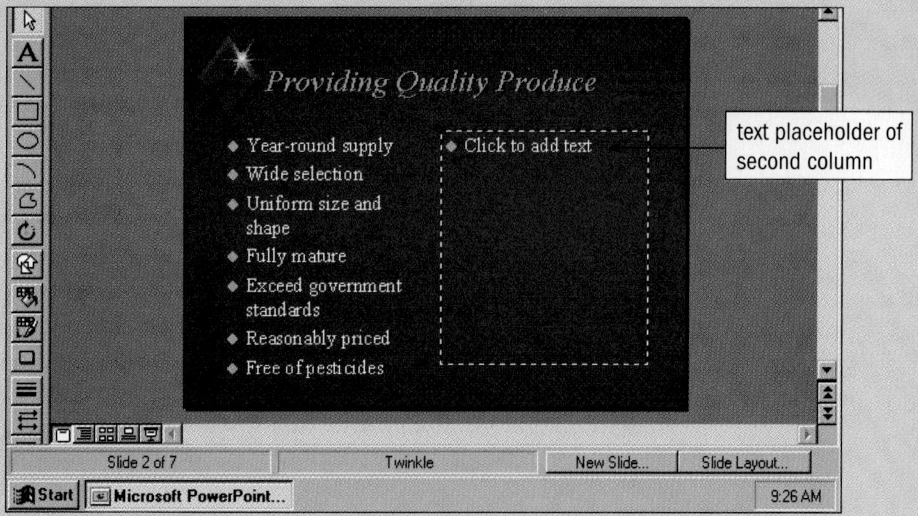

text placeholder of
second column

Now you can add the new item to the bulleted list.

To add new text to a text placeholder:

1. Click anywhere within the text placeholder that says "Click to add text." PowerPoint removes the message that was there, displays a bullet, and positions the insertion point to the right of the bullet.

2. Type **Hand picked** and press the **Enter** key. A second bullet is added. Now Enrique wants you to move the last three items in the first column to the end of the second column so the columns are balanced.

3. Click anywhere on the text in the first column. The text box becomes selected. If necessary, scroll down so you can see the last three items in the first column.

4. Position the pointer over the bullet next to "Exceed government standards." The pointer changes to ⊕.

5. Click the mouse button, then press and hold the **Shift** key, click the bullets next to "Reasonably priced" and "Free of pesticides," and release the **Shift** key to select all of the items you want to move at once.

6. Click the **Cut** button ✂ on the Standard toolbar. The text disappears from the screen and is moved to the clipboard.

7. Click I just to the right of the second bullet in the second column, then click the **Paste** button 📋 on the Standard toolbar. The three cut items appear in the second column. See Figure 3-12. You have completed slide 2 of Enrique's presentation.

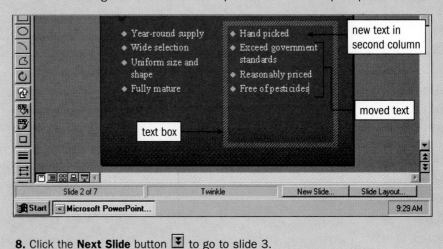

Figure 3-12 ◀
Slide after
moving text

8. Click the **Next Slide** button ⬇ to go to slide 3.

Slide 2 contains the additional text that Enrique wanted and has a two-column design to accommodate the new text in an attractive and readable way. Now you're ready to edit slide 3.

Inserting Clip Art

Slide 3, "Meeting Your Needs," has four items of information. Enrique wants to include some clip art to add interest to this slide. In PowerPoint, **clip art** specifically refers to images in the Microsoft ClipArt Gallery, whereas a **picture** is any image from some other source, including clip-art libraries supplied by other companies.

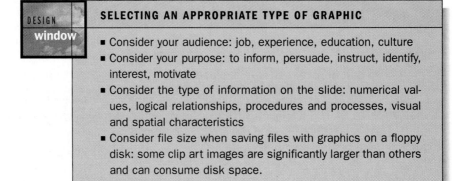

DESIGN
window

SELECTING AN APPROPRIATE TYPE OF GRAPHIC

■ Consider your audience: job, experience, education, culture
■ Consider your purpose: to inform, persuade, instruct, identify, interest, motivate
■ Consider the type of information on the slide: numerical values, logical relationships, procedures and processes, visual and spatial characteristics
■ Consider file size when saving files with graphics on a floppy disk: some clip art images are significantly larger than others and can consume disk space.

Let's now change the layout of the slide and add clip art to it.

To change the layout of the slide and add clip art:

1. With slide 3 showing in Slide View, click the **Slide Layout** button on the status bar to display the Slide Layout dialog box, click the layout with the description **Text & Clip Art**, then click the **Apply** button to change the layout of the slide. See Figure 3-13.

Figure 3-13 ◀
Slide with
new layout

2. Double-click the **clip art** placeholder. PowerPoint displays the Microsoft ClipArt Gallery dialog box. See Figure 3-14.

Figure 3-14 ◀
Microsoft
ClipArt Gallery
window

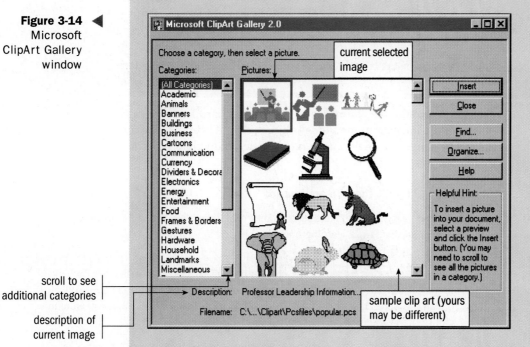

TROUBLE? If PowerPoint displays a ClipArt Gallery dialog box that tells you it may take a few minutes for the ClipArt Gallery to create the list of pictures, click the OK button. PowerPoint will automatically set up its built-in clip-art library.

3. Scroll the "Categories " list box until you see "People," then click **People** to select that category.

TROUBLE? If you don't see a list of categories for the clip-art library, or if the clip art is missing altogether, consult your instructor or technical support person. If you do have clip art to choose from, but you don't have the People category, choose any clip art you prefer to complete these steps.

4. If necessary, scroll the clip-art images within the People category until you see the image of a woman standing by a blackboard with a group of four people sitting in front of her, then click that image. See Figure 3-15. The clip-art title at the bottom of the dialog box gives the description of the image, "Leadership."

Figure 3-15 ◀
ClipArt Gallery
window with
new image
selected

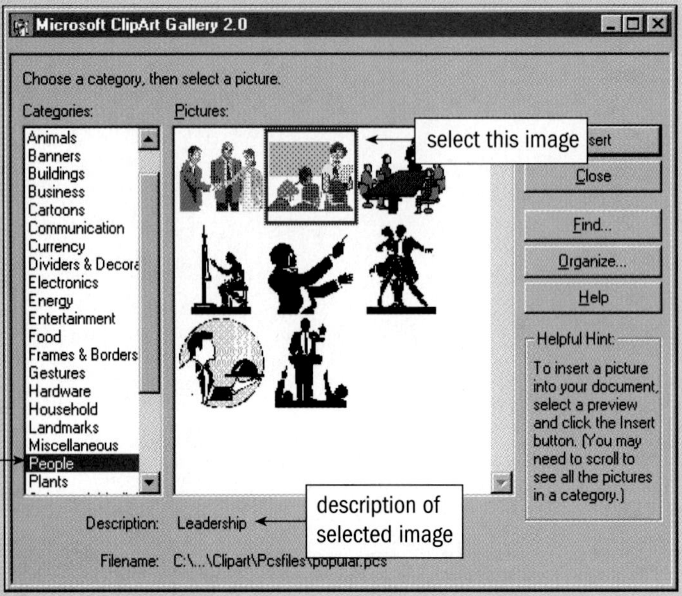

current category ——————→

5. Click the **Insert** button. The clip art is inserted into the slide.

Enrique would like you to remove the blackboard from the figure. To do this, you will ungroup the image into individual objects, then delete the blackboard object. To **ungroup** means to convert a single image into smaller, individual objects. Let's ungroup and edit the image now.

To ungroup and edit the clip-art image:

1. With the Leadership image still selected, click **Draw** and then click **Ungroup**. PowerPoint displays a warning about discarding any embedded data or linking information.

2. Click the **OK** button because this clip art has no special embedded data or linking information. (A graph from a spreadsheet, which might be modified if you change the spreadsheet data, would contain linking information that you wouldn't want to break.) Resize handles appear around the various objects in the picture.

3. Click in a blank area of the slide to deselect all objects, then click the blackboard behind the woman. The image of the blackboard is selected, but not the people in the image.

   TROUBLE? If you didn't use the Leadership clip-art image, your image may not be able to ungroup, or if it does ungroup, you may not be able to select one of the items individually. If this occurs, skip to Step 5.

4. Press the **Delete** key to delete the selected object. The blackboard disappears from the slide. You have now completed slide 3 of Enrique's presentation. See Figure 3-16.

Figure 3-16 ◀
Slide with
clip art

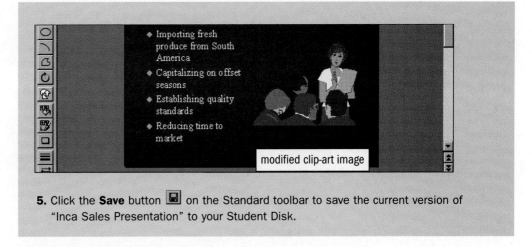

modified clip-art image

5. Click the **Save** button  on the Standard toolbar to save the current version of "Inca Sales Presentation" to your Student Disk.

This concludes Session 3.1. You can exit PowerPoint or continue to the next session.

Quick Check

1. Describe how to do the following:
   a. Select a text box so that resize handles appear
   b. Change the size of a text box
   c. Move a text box on a slide
   d. Change the alignment of a text box from center to left alignment

2. How would you do each of the following?
   a. Insert a picture into a slide
   b. Change the layout of an existing slide
   c. Insert a clip-art image into a slide
   d. Remove background graphics from a slide

3. List four situations in which you could use graphics effectively.

4. Why would you ungroup a clip-art image?

5. Explain the meaning of the following terms:
   a. Slide Layout
   b. clip art
   c. object
   d. resize handles

6. List three principles for selecting an appropriate type of graphic.

SESSION
3.2

In this session you'll learn how to create graphs and organizational charts for your slide presentations.

Inserting a Graph

On slide 4 of the presentation, Enrique wants you to add a column chart that compares Inca Imports International's time to market (that is, the time from picking to customer delivery, in hours) during the past four quarters with that of the other two major produce import companies in Southern California.

INSERTING A COLUMN CHART

- Display the desired slide in Slide View.
- If necessary, change the Slide Layout to "Text & Graph" or "Graph & Text."
- Double-click the area marked "Double click to add graph." PowerPoint displays a datasheet.
- Edit the information in the datasheet for the data that you want to plot.
- Click anywhere outside the datasheet, then click anywhere outside the graph box.

Let's add the graph now.

To add a column chart to the slide:

1. If necessary, start PowerPoint and open the file "Inca Sales Presentation" from your Student Disk and then go to slide 4, "Reducing Time to Market."

2. Click the **Slide Layout** button on the status bar, click the layout with the name **Text & Graph** (it's usually the picture in the second row in the first column), then click the **Apply** button. The text on the slide becomes formatted into a smaller text box on the left side of the slide, and a graph box placeholder appears on the right side.

3. Double-click the **graph box** placeholder. After few moments, PowerPoint inserts a sample graph and displays a **datasheet**, or a grid of cells, similar to a Microsoft Excel worksheet, in which you can add data and labels.

   TROUBLE? Don't worry if the colors on the slide become distorted. They'll return to normal once you close the datasheet window.

   To create your own graph you simply change the information in the sample datasheet on the screen. The information on the datasheet is stored in **cells**, which are the little boxes that contain a number, word, or phrase. The cells are organized into rows and columns. The rows are numbered 1, 2, 3..., and the columns are labeled A, B, C.... You'll edit the information in the datasheet to reflect the three companies' times to market. Let's do that now.

To edit the information in the datasheet:

1. Position the pointer over the cell that contains the word "East." The pointer changes to ✛.

2. Click the cell that contains the word "East," and type **SCP** (which stands for "Southern California Produce," one of Inca Imports' major competitors).

3. Press the **Down Arrow** key to select the cell labeled "West," then type **CCF** (which stands for "Central City Foods," Inca Imports' other major competitor).

4. Repeat Step 3 to replace "North" with **Inca**. See Figure 3-17. Now you're ready to change the actual numbers in the datasheet.

Figure 3-17
Slide with
graph

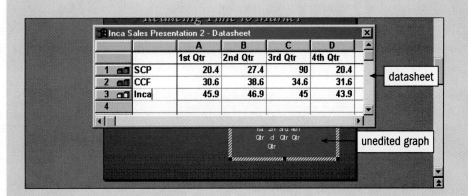

5. Click cell **A1**, the cell at which column A and row 1 intersect, then type **18**. This is SCP's average time to market in hours during the first quarter of the year.

6. Press the **Tab** key or the **Right Arrow** key to select cell **B1**, type **27**, press the **Tab** key, type **22**, press the **Tab** key, then type **20**. This completes the data for SCP.

7. Using the same procedure as in Steps 5 and 6, replace the current data for CCF and for Inca, using the data shown in Figure 3-18. Carefully check the datasheet to make sure it matches Figure 3-18. Make any necessary corrections.

Figure 3-18
Completed
datasheet

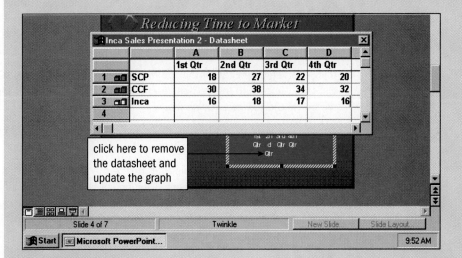

8. Click anywhere outside the datasheet but still within the graph box behind the datasheet (for example, in the lower-right corner of the graph box) to remove the datasheet from the screen. The completed graph appears on the screen.

TROUBLE? If you accidentally click outside the graph box, the dashed box around the graph will disappear, and only the resize handles will still show around the selected graph. Double-click the graph to return to the mode for editing the graph.

Now Enrique wants you to insert a title to label the vertical axis of the graph. Let's do that now.

To insert a title into a graph:

1. Click **Insert**, then click **Titles** to open the Titles dialog box.

TROUBLE? If you don't see Titles on the Insert menu, double-click the graph to return to the mode for editing the graph.

2. Click the **Value (Z) Axis** check box, then click the **OK** button. PowerPoint displays a small text box to the left of the vertical axis with the letter "Z" as its contents.

3. Double-click the lower–left resize handle of the **Z-axis title**. The Format Axis Title dialog box appears on the screen. See Figure 3-19.

Figure 3-19 ◀
Format Axis
Title dialog box

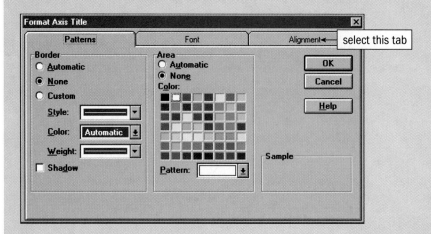

TROUBLE? If you clicked or double-clicked inside the text box, the resize handles disappear. Click within the graph box but outside any other object in the box (for example, in the lower-right corner of the graph box), then double-click the Z-axis title. If the Format Plot Area dialog box appears as a result of Step 3, click the Cancel button, then follow the steps described in this TROUBLE? paragraph.

4. Click the **Alignment** tab at the top of the dialog box, then in the Orientation box click the "Text" with the vertical orientation (it reads bottom to top). It's the middle box in the row of three boxes.

5. Click the **OK** button to return to the graph on the slide. The "Z" on the vertical axis is now rotated so it reads bottom to top.

6. Click I on the "**Z**" in the Z-axis title, delete the Z (for example, by pressing the **Backspace** key), then type **Hours**. This indicates that graphed time from picking to delivery is in hours. Click anywhere within the graph box but outside other objects to deselect the title. Notice that some or all of the labels along the X-axis (for example, the word "2nd") are split in two; to fix this you must increase the width of the graph to allow more room for the text.

7. Position the pointer over the left center resize handle of the graph box, so that the pointer changes to ↔, then drag the handle to the left until the left edge of the graph box is near the right edge of the text of the slide. See Figure 3-20.

Figure 3-20 ◀
Completed
graph after
resizing

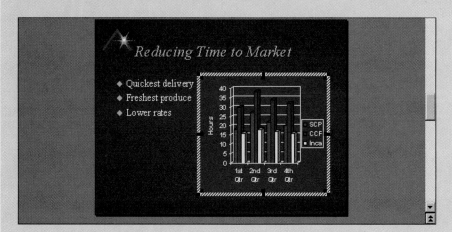

TROUBLE? If the graph box won't move to the left as indicated in Step 7, you may have selected the graph instead of the graph box. Click Edit, then click Undo Size and try Step 7 again.

TROUBLE? If your graph doesn't look like Figure 3-20, click the View Datasheet button on the Graph toolbar to display the datasheet. Make the necessary revisions by comparing your datasheet with Figure 3-18.

You have now completed slide 4 of Enrique's presentation. Let's deselect the graph and go to the next slide.

To deselect the graph:

1. Click twice outside the graph area—once to exit graph mode and once to deselect the graph.

Inserting an Organization Chart

Because Inca Imports is a fairly new company, Enrique and his staff feel that it's important for potential clients to understand Inca employees' high level of experience in the import and produce businesses. Enrique therefore asks you to create an organization chart to communicate this. An **organization chart** is a diagram of boxes, connected together with lines, showing the hierarchy of positions within an organization. Let's create the organization chart now.

REFERENCE
window

INSERTING AN ORGANIZATION CHART

- Change the Slide Layout of the desired slide to Organization Chart.
- Double-click the organization chart placeholder.
- Type the personnel names, positions, and other information into the boxes of the organization chart.
- Add subordinate and co-worker boxes as desired.
- Click File, click Exit and Return to (presentation name), then click the Yes button.

To create an organization chart:

1. Go to slide 5, click the **Slide Layout** button on the status bar, click the layout with the name **Organization Chart**, and click the **Apply** button.

2. Double-click the **org chart** placeholder. After a few moments, the Microsoft Organization Chart window appears on the screen with the Organization Chart toolbar across the top.

3. Click the **Maximize** button on the Organization Chart window so it will fill the entire screen. See Figure 3-21. A chart with text placeholders appears in the window. The chart has two levels of organization. The first line in the box at the top of the chart is already selected, as you can tell from its dark background. When you start typing, the text will appear in that selected box.

Figure 3-21 ◀
Microsoft
Organization
Chart window

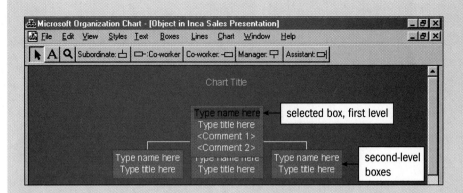

4. Type **Patricia Cuevas** on the first line.

5. Press the **Tab** key or the **Enter** key. The placeholder text "Your Title here" becomes selected.

6. Type **President**, press the **Tab** key, and type **13 years' experience**. This completes the first box. PowerPoint will automatically delete the fourth (extra) line for you if you don't use it.

7. Click the second-level box on the left side. The box becomes selected, as shown by its black background.

8. Type **Angelena Cristenas**, press the **Tab** key, type **V.P. Operations**, press the **Tab** key, and type **13 years' experience**. This completes the text of that text box in the organization chart.

9. Using the same procedure as in Steps 6 and 7, complete the other two boxes of the organization chart, so they contain the text shown in Figure 3-22, then click anywhere within the Microsoft Organization Chart window, but outside of any text or organization box, to take the chart out of editing mode.

Figure 3-22 ◀
First two levels
of Organization
Chart

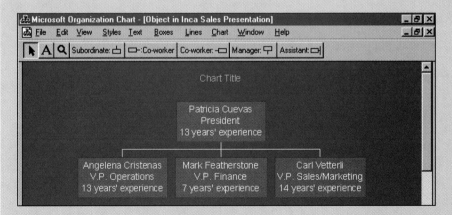

TROUBLE? If you made any typing errors, click the box containing the error, then press the Tab key until the line containing the error is highlighted, then retype that line.

You have completed the first two levels of the organization chart. Enrique also wants to show the experience personnel at Inca Imports have in handling produce and responding to customer delivery needs. The customer service employees work under Angelena Cristenas. Let's add the new levels of organization now.

To add subordinate levels to an organization chart:

1. Click the **Subordinate** button Subordinate: ⤴ on the Organization Chart toolbar. The pointer changes to ⤴ .

2. Click anywhere within the box containing "Angelena Cristenas." A new organization level appears below Angelena's box. See Figure 3-23. The small black box within the new box indicates that the new box is selected and ready for you to type new text.

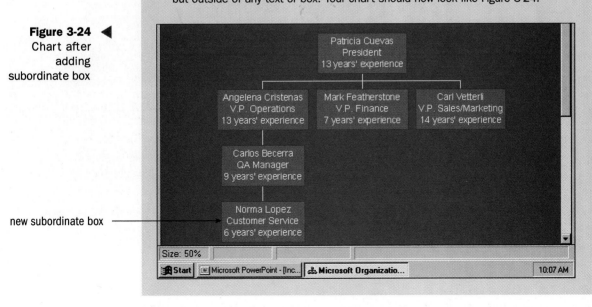

Figure 3-23 ◀
New organization level

Subordinate button ——

new third-level subordinate box

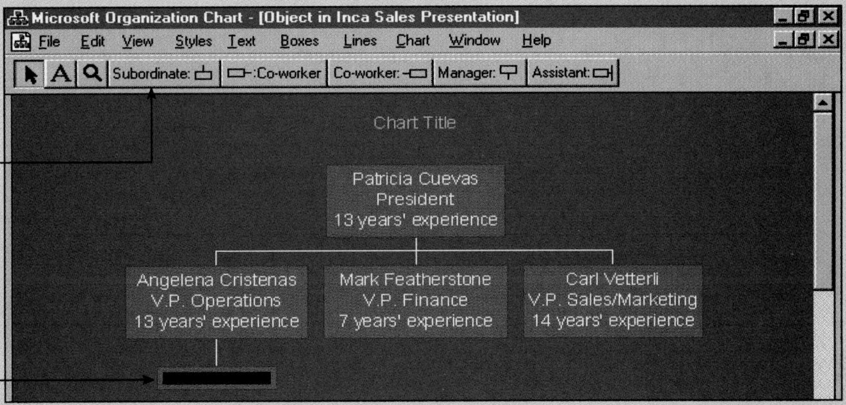

3. Type **Carlos Becerra**. As soon as you begin to type, the other text placeholders appear in the box.

4. Press the **Tab** key, type **QA Manager**, press the **Tab** key, and type **9 years' experience**. This completes the box for Carlos Becerra, QA (quality assurance) manager.

5. Click Subordinate: ⤴ and click the box containing "Carlos Becerra" to add a subordinate box underneath Carlos.

6. Type **Norma Lopez**, press the **Tab** key, type **Customer Service**, press the **Tab** key, and type **6 years' experience**, then click anywhere in the Organization Chart window, but outside of any text or box. Your chart should now look like Figure 3-24.

Figure 3-24 ◀
Chart after adding subordinate box

new subordinate box ——

Enrique wants you to add a co-worker to the chart. Let's do that now.

To add a co-worker to an organization chart:

1. Click the **Right Co-worker** button on the Organization Chart toolbar. The mouse changes to ⌐. This allows you to add a co-worker box to the right of an existing box.

2. Click the box containing "**Norma Lopez**" to add a new box to its right, type **Juanita Rojas**, press the **Tab** key, type **Manager, Quito Center**, press the **Tab** key, type **3 years' experience**, and click anywhere in the window, but outside of any box or text, to take the chart out of editing mode.

You have completed the organization chart. Now you need to exit the Organization Chart window to add it to the slide.

To exit the Organization Chart window and add the chart to the slide:

1. Click **File**, then click **Exit and Return to Inca Sales Presentation**. A dialog box appears on the screen asking if you want to update the object. The object in this case is the new organization chart.

2. Click the **Yes** button. After looking over the organization chart, Enrique asks you to make it bigger.

3. Drag the resize handle in the upper-left corner up and to the left, then drag the resize handle in the lower-right corner down and to the right until the organization chart is approximately the same size as the one shown in Figure 3-25.

Figure 3-25 ◀
Completed
organization
chart

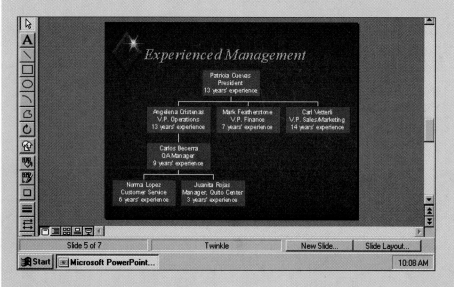

4. Click anywhere outside the selected organization chart to deselect it. Slide 5 now looks like Figure 3-25. You have completed the first five slides in Enrique's presentation.

5. Click the **Save** button 🖫 on the Standard toolbar to save the presentation using the current filename.

Quick Check

1. How would you create a graph in a slide?

2. How would you add an organization chart to a slide?

3. In the context of an organization chart, define the following:
   a. subordinate
   b. co-worker

4. What is an organization chart?

5. In creating a graph, what is a datasheet?

6. In a datasheet, what are the two methods (one using the keyboard, the other using the mouse) to move from one cell to the next?

This concludes Session 3.2. You can exit PowerPoint or continue to the next session.

SESSION

3.3

In this session you'll learn how to draw and manipulate graphic shapes.

Creating and Manipulating a Shape

Enrique wants you to add a simple drawing with text to slide 6 to demonstrate the three major benefits of the company. To do this, Enrique wants you to insert an inverted triangle in the slide. Let's do that now.

To insert a shape in a slide:

1. If necessary, open the file "Inca Sales Presentation" on your Student Disk. Go to slide 6, then click the **AutoShapes** button  on the Drawing toolbar. PowerPoint displays the AutoShapes palette. See Figure 3-26.

Figure 3-26
AutoShapes
palette

AutoShapes button
on Draw toolbar

Isosceles triangle tool

AutoShapes palette

2. Click the **Isosceles Triangle Tool** button ⬜ on the AutoShapes palette. When you move the pointer into the slide, the pointer changes to ✛.

3. Position ✛ approximately one inch below the second "n" in "International" (in the title of the slide), then click the mouse button and drag the pointer down and to the right. The outline of a triangle appears as you drag.

4. Release the mouse button when your triangle is approximately the same size and shape as the one in Figure 3-27.

Figure 3-27 ◀
Slide with
drawn triangle

graphic object ──

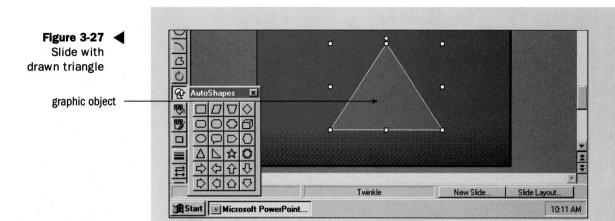

5. Click the **Close** button ⊠ in the upper-right corner of the AutoShapes palette to close the palette. It disappears from the screen.

   TROUBLE? If your triangle doesn't look like the one in Figure 3-27, you can move your triangle by dragging it to a new location; you can resize or change the shape of your triangle by dragging one or more of the resize handles; or you can press the Backspace key to delete your triangle and repeat Steps 1 through 5 to redraw the triangle.

   Notice that the default color of the drawn object is pink. You decide that pink is too bright and want to change the color of the triangle to cyan (blue-green), which matches the color of the text on the slide.

6. With the triangle still selected, click **Format**, then click **Colors and Lines**. The Colors and Lines dialog box appears on the screen.

7. Click the Fill list arrow, click the **cyan** tile (the second tile in the second row), then click the **OK** button.

The triangle is the desired size and color, but you want to flip the triangle so it is pointing down instead of up. Let's flip the triangle now.

To flip an object:

1. With the triangle still selected, click **Draw**, click **Rotate/Flip**, and then click **Flip Vertical**.

2. Click in a blank region of the slide to deselect the triangle.

   Your triangle should be positioned, colored, sized, and oriented like the one shown in Figure 3-28.

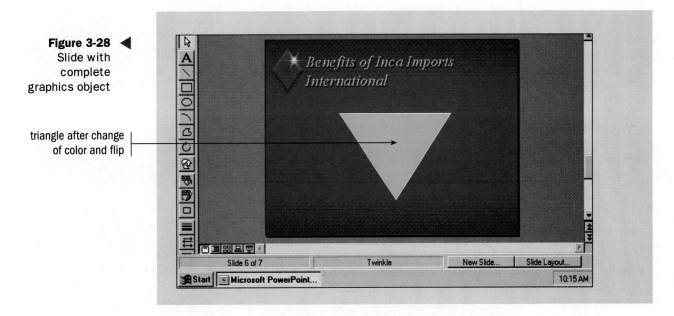

Figure 3-28 ◀
Slide with
complete
graphics object

triangle after change
of color and flip

The shape is now in its final form.

Adding a Text Box

You are ready to add the text naming the three benefits of Inca Imports on each side of the triangle. Let's do that now.

To add a text box to the slide:

1. Click the **Text Tool** button [A] on the Drawing toolbar. The pointer changes to ↓.

2. Move the pointer so it is just above the upper-left corner of the triangle and click at that position. PowerPoint creates a small empty text box, with the insertion point inside.

3. Type **Quality Produce**.

4. Click anywhere on the edge of the text box to select it. Resize handles will appear around the text box.

5. Drag the edge of the text box until it is positioned just above and centered on the upper edge of the triangle, as shown in Figure 3-29.

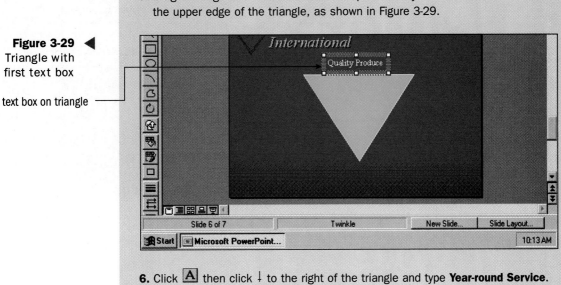

Figure 3-29 ◀
Triangle with
first text box

text box on triangle

6. Click [A] then click ↓ to the right of the triangle and type **Year-round Service**.

7. Click **A** then click ↓ to the left of the triangle and type **Satisfied Customers**. Click in a blank area of the slide to deselect the text box. Your slide should now look like Figure 3-30. Don't worry if the text you added to the sides of the triangle is not in the same position as the text in the figure. You will move the text boxes in the next set of steps.

Figure 3-30 ◄
Triangle with additional text boxes

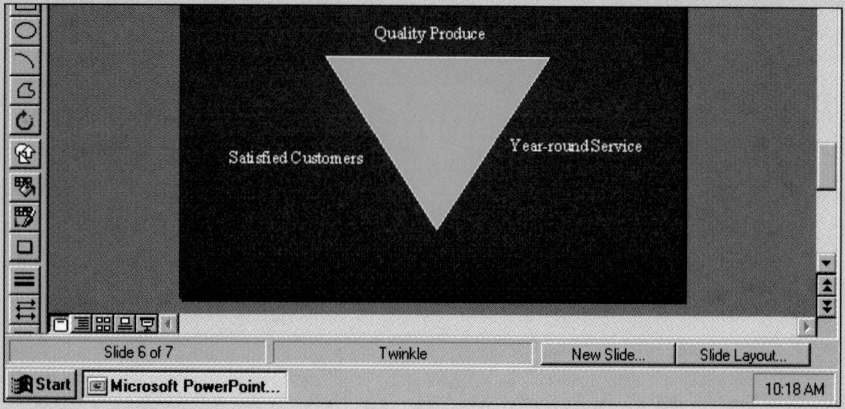

Now you'll rotate the text boxes to make them parallel to the sides of the triangle. The method for rotating text is similar to the one for rotating graphics (or rotating any other object).

To rotate and move the text boxes:

1. Select the text box that contains "Year-round Service" by clicking anywhere within the box, then clicking the edge of the box. The resize handles appear around the box.

2. Click the **Free Rotate Tool** button on the Drawing toolbar. The pointer changes to .

3. Position the over one of the resize handles (it doesn't matter which one). The pointer changes again, this time to .

4. Press and hold the mouse button.

5. Rotate the handle counterclockwise until the status bar indicates that you have rotated the box about 60 degrees or until the top edge of the box is parallel to the lower-right edge of the triangle. See Figure 3-31.

Figure 3-31 ◄
Slide while rotating text

rotated text

rotate pointer

current rotation angle

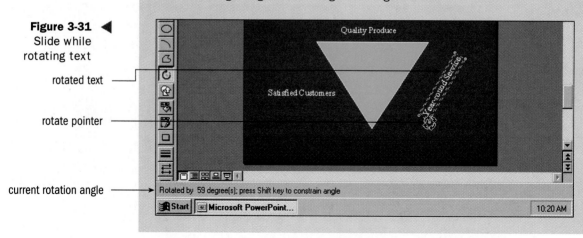

6. Click the **Selection Tool** button ▷ on the Drawing toolbar, then select the "Year-round Service" text box. The first time you click the text, it flips so it is vertical or horizontal. Click the edge of the text box to select it, and the text will return to its rotated position.

7. Drag the edge of the text box until it is close to and centered on the lower-right edge of the triangle.

   TROUBLE? If the edge of the text box isn't parallel to the edge of the triangle, you can repeat Steps 2 through 5 above to fix the rotation.

8. Click the text box that contains "Satisfied Customers," then repeat Steps 2 through 7, except this time rotate the box clockwise to about 300 degrees or until it is parallel to the lower-left edge of the triangle, then position the text box so it is close to and centered on the left edge of the triangle. Deselect the text box. Your slide should look like Figure 3-32.

Figure 3-32 ◀
Slide with completed diagram

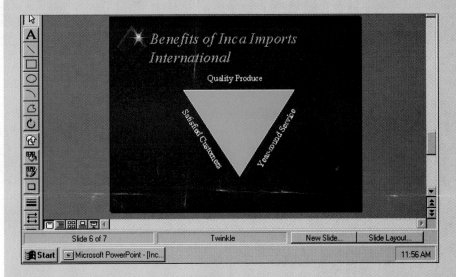

You have now completed the entire presentation, so you should save the final version to the disk.

9. With the Student Disk still in the disk drive, click the **Save** button 🖫. PowerPoint saves the file using its current filename.

A copy of the updated presentation is now on your Student Disk.

Viewing and Printing the Completed Slide Show

You should view the completed slide show before you print it.

To view the completed presentation as a slide show:

1. Drag the **scroll box** to the top of the vertical scroll bar so slide 1 will appear first when you begin the slide show.

2. Click the **Slide Show** button 🖳 on the View toolbar to begin the slide show.

3. After you look at each slide, click the left mouse button or press the **spacebar** to advance to the next slide. Continue advancing until you've seen the entire slide show and PowerPoint returns to Slide View.

4. Click the **Slide Sorter View** button ▦ to see at least the first six slides at once. Your completed presentation should look like Figure 3-33. Before printing the slides on a black-and-white printer, you should preview the slides in black and white.

Figure 3-33 ◀
Complete slide
presentation

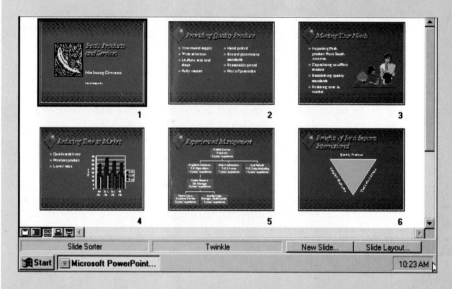

5. While still in Slide Sorter View, click the **B&W View** button 🖼 on the Formatting toolbar. The slides change from color to black and white. As you can see, all the slides are legible in black and white.

Enrique and his staff would like a hard copy of the presentation for their files. You can now print the presentation by selecting Slides in the Print dialog box, then selecting the Black & White check box to print the slides on your printer.

Quick Check

1 How would you draw a shape such as a rectangle or a circle?

2 What is the AutoShape feature?

3 How would you change the fill color of a shape?

4 How would you invert a triangle so it is pointed down instead of up?

5 How would you rotate an object (a text box or a graphics image)?

Tutorial Assignments

In the following Tutorial Assignments, make sure you click the Open an Existing File button when you start PowerPoint or, if PowerPoint is already running, click the Open button on the Standard toolbar, then open each file. After working with a presentation and saving your changes, close the presentation.

Open the file Report from the TAssign folder on your Student Disk and do the following:

1. Save the file to your Student Disk as Marketing Report.
2. Make sure that slide 1 appears in the presentation window in Slide View.
3. Change the text in both text boxes to Left Alignment so that the text is flush with the left edge of the text boxes. *Hint*: Select the text, then click the Left Alignment button on the Formatting toolbar.
4. Decrease the size of each of the two text boxes so that they fit just around the text contained in each box.

5. Move the two text boxes so that their right edges are near the right edge of the slide.
6. Using the Align command on the Draw menu, adjust the two text boxes so their left edges are aligned.
7. Insert the picture file Incalogo from your Student Disk into slide 1, decrease the size of the logo by approximately 50%, then move the picture just to the left of the title, just above the colored double line.
8. Change the layout of slide 2 to "2 Column Text."
9. In the right column of slide 2, add the following three bulleted items: "Ad in food industry trade magazine," "Sample produce to interested businesses," "Complimentary shipment to large companies."
10. In slide 3 change the layout to "Clip Art & Text," so that the clip art is on the left and the text is on the right.
11. In the placeholder for the clip art in slide 3, add the image from the People category called "Consensus," which pictures a man and a woman shaking hands with another man watching. If your copy of PowerPoint doesn't have that clip-art image, use another one of your choice and skip step 12.

12. Ungroup the clip-art image and remove the man standing in the middle.
13. Add an organization chart to slide 4. Add Enrique Hoffmann, Director of Marketing, at the top of the chart. Add Melanie Zapatos and Samuel Clarke, both Marketing Managers, to the second level. Then, on the third level under Melanie Zapatos, add two Sales Representatives (as co-workers, Carlos Anderson and Ana Maria Prado); under Samuel Clarke add two Sales Representatives (as co-workers, Gina Parker and Jesus Calderon). *Hint:* To delete an unwanted box in the organization chart, select the box, then press the Backspace or the Delete key.

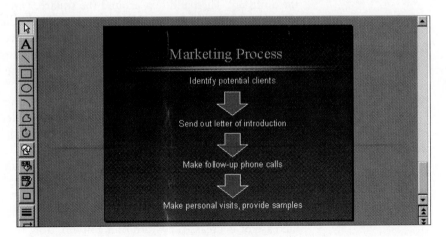

14. Add a new slide 5. Choose "Title Only" as the slide layout. Make the title of the slide "Marketing Process." Add text and AutoShapes to create a slide that looks like Figure 3-34. You may have to move, resize, and align text and graphics boxes to make the slide look right. *Hint:* To make the arrows the same size and shape, use AutoShapes to draw one of the arrows and then use the Copy and Paste buttons on the Standard toolbar to create the others. To align the centers of objects vertically (text boxes and graphics boxes), use the Draw, Align, Centers command.

Figure 3-34 ◀

15. Add a new slide 6. Choose "Graph" as the slide layout. Make the title of the slide "Comparison of 4th Qtr Sales, 1992-95." Double-click the graph icon and then in the datasheet, delete the second and third rows. *Hint:* Click the gray box labeled 2, click Edit, and click Delete to delete the entire row. Change labels in columns A through D from "1st Qtr," "2nd Qtr," and so forth, to "1992," "1993," "1994," and "1995." Change the label in row 1 from "East" to "4th Qtr Sales." Enter the following data into cells A1 through D1: $420, $475, $710, $1025. Add the title "Thousands" to the Z-axis; make the title vertical (reading bottom to top). Close the datasheet and then deselect the graph.

16. Check the spelling within the presentation by clicking the Spelling button on the Standard toolbar or click Tools, then click Spelling.

17. View the entire presentation in Slide Show View and in Black-and-White View.

18. Save the file with your changes, then print a copy of the slides (three slides per page) of the presentation. Print them using the Black & White option if you don't have a color printer.

19. Close the file.
   Open the file Service from the TAssign folder on your Student Disk and do the following:

20. Save it to your Student Disk as Customer Service.

21. Make sure that PowerPoint is in Slide View and that slide 1 appears in the presentation window.

22. Insert the picture file Design from the TAssign folder on your Student Disk into slide 1, then position the picture so it is centered below the author's name, "Norma Lopez."

23. Remove the Slide Master objects from this title slide.

24. Change the layout of slide 2 to "2 Column Text."

25. In the right column of slide 2, add the following two bulleted items: "Hold customer training" and "Improve product list."

26. Move the fourth item from column 1 to be the last item of column 2.

27. In slide 3 change the layout to "Text & Clip Art," so the clip art is on the right and the text is on the left; then in the placeholder for the clip art, add the image from the "People" category that shows a man and a woman shaking hands with another man, watching. If your copy of PowerPoint doesn't have that clip-art image, use another one of your choice.

28. Create an organization chart in slide 4. Put Norma Lopez, Customer Service, at the top of the chart, with Delbert Green as her assistant on level 2, and three people, Shirley Alvarez, Daniel Truong, and Whitney Sanders, all Customer Representatives, on level 3 below Delbert Green. *Hint:* To delete an unwanted box on the organization chart, select the box, then press the Backspace or the Delete key.

29. Go to slide 5 and add a square in the middle of the slide that is about one-fourth the width of the slide. *Hint:* Use the Rectangle Tool while holding down the Shift key. Then add text around the square. *Hint*: Use the Free Rotate Tool to rotate the text that goes along the left and right sides, but don't rotate the text that goes along the top or bottom of the square. Type "Quality Products" above the box, "Quick Response" along the right edge (rotated 270 degrees), "Honored Guarantees" along the bottom, and "Regular Follow-up" along the left edge (rotated 90 degrees).

30. Change the fill color of the rectangle to cyan (blue-green).

31. Go to slide 6 and double-click the placeholder labeled "Double click to add graph." Click the down arrow immediately to the right of the Chart Type button on the toolbar to display icons of the various chart types. Click the three-dimensional pie chart (on the fifth row, second column). On the datasheet, change the column labels from "1st Qtr," "2nd Qtr," and so forth, to "Extremely Satisfied," "Very Satisfied," "Satisfied," and "Unsatisfied." *Hint*: You may have to change the width of the columns for these labels to fit. To increase or decrease the width of a column, drag the black line located between the gray column buttons along the top of the datasheet to the left or the right. Beneath those labels enter the following data into cells A1 through D1: 0.31, 0.42, 0.25, and 0.02, respectively, to indicate the percent of customers in each category. Close the datasheet and deselect the pie chart.

32. View the entire presentation in Slide Show View.

33. Save the file with your changes.

34. Print a copy of the slides (as four slides per page) of the presentation. Print them using the Black & White option if you don't have a color printer.

35. Close the file.

Case Problems

1. Data Doctor Enoch Norbert owns a computer-data-backup service in Framingham, Massachusetts. His company, Data Doctor, helps small businesses in the greater Boston area back up their disks and recover damaged data. Enoch wants to use PowerPoint to create a presentation for potential customers.

Open the file presentation Datadoc from the Cases folder on your Student Disk, save it as Case 1 - Data Doctor, then do the following:

1. To slide 1, add the picture Datalogo from the Cases folder on your Student Disk. Adjust the position and alignment of the text and the position of the picture to make the slide attractive and readable.

2. In slide 3, add the PowerPoint clip art showing a duck smashing a PC (also having the description "Stress Frustration Anger") from the Cartoons category. If your copy of PowerPoint doesn't have this clip-art image or the ones that follow, use another one of your choice.

3. In slide 4, add to the center of the slide (below the title) the clip art with the description "Future Forecast" from the Cartoons category.

4. Also in slide 4, add a text box with the text "Data Doctor." Center the text box below the clip-art image.

5. Change the layout of slide 6 to Graph & Text. In the graph area, create a graph that compares restore costs (from backed-up data) and reenter costs (from loss of data). In the datasheet, title columns A through D as follows: "1 hr," "8 hrs," "20 hrs," and "40 hrs" (the restoration times in hours). Then title rows 1 and 2 as follows: "Off-site" and "On-site." Delete any other rows. In the "Off-site" row (cells A1 through D1) enter the costs for restoring from an off-site backup: 3, 24, 60, 120. In the "On-site" row (cells A2 through D2) type the costs for restoring from an on-site backup: 10, 80, 200, 400. Add a vertical label to the Z-axis: "Cost in dollars." If the words in the X-axis labels wrap unattractively, increase the width of the graph. You may also need to change the size of the text box to the right of the graph so the graph doesn't cover up the text.

6. In slide 7, increase the size of the font in the main text box (below the title) by selecting the text box and dragging the I-beam pointer over all the text and then clicking the Increase Font Size button five or six times until the longest line of text just fills the width of the text box.

7. Use Slide Show to view all the slides of the presentation, then save the file.

8. View all the slides of the presentation in black and white. Because the diagonal bars show up as a dark gray, the text on the slides is hard to read. To solve the problem, omit the background graphics from all the slides in the presentation.

9. Print the slides of the presentation in black and white as four slides per page.

10. Close the file without saving the changes. You don't want to omit the background graphics from your saved version of the presentation.

2. Business Plans Plus Atu Hemuli helps minority entrepreneurs obtain funding by preparing business plans for them or by editing their existing plans. Atu wants to create a seminar presentation for other professionals who are interested in becoming business-plan consultants.

Open the file presentation Busplans from the Cases folder on your Student Disk and save it as Case 2 - Business Plans Plus and do the following:

1. Insert a new slide 2 into the presentation. Use the "Bulleted List" slide layout. Add the title "What does a business plan consultant do?" Then add the following bulleted items to the main text: "Guides clients in writing business plans," "Conducts market research," "Gathers financial information," "Projects growth," and "Projects sales potential."

2. Change the layout for slide 3 (formerly slide 2) to Text & Graph. Add a pie chart in the graphic box. *Hint*: After double-clicking the graph icon, click the down arrow to the right of the Chart Type button, then click the pie chart icon (on the fifth row, first column). On the datasheet, change the column labels from "1st Qtr" and "2nd Qtr" to "Formal Business Plan" and "No Business Plan." Delete the labels and information in the other columns. Beneath the column labels, edit into cells A1 and B1 the data 0.59 and 0.41, respectively, to indicate the percentage in each category. Close the datasheet and deselect the pie chart. You may need to resize the graph box if the words wrap.
3. In slide 4, add a pie chart similar to the one in slide 3, except the data in cells A1 and B1 should be 0.42 and 0.58, respectively.
4. In slide 5, add a pie chart similar to the one in slide 3, except create three column labels: "No planning," "Some planning," and "Formal planning." Then make the label in row one "Planning." Enter into cells A1, B1, and C1 the data 30, 45, and 25, respectively.
5. Change the layout of slide 6 to Text & Clip Art, then add any one of the clip-art images of a handshake from the Gestures category. If your copy of PowerPoint doesn't have this clip-art image or the ones that follow, use another one of your choice.
6. Change the layout of slide 7 to Text & Clip Art, then add a different clip-art image of a handshake from the Gestures category.
7. Use Slide Show to review the entire presentation.
8. Save the file, then print the slides in black and white as four slides per page.
9. Close the file.

3. Porter and Coles Ad Agency Sheri Porter and Sherone Coles are partners who founded the Porter and Coles Ad Agency. They decide to prepare a presentation to provide potential clients with the hourly rates for Porter and Coles' services and provide a graph on the costs of preparing a document as a function of the number of pages.

Open the file presentation Porter from the Cases folder on your Student Disk and save it as Case 3 - Porter and Coles, then do the following:

1. In slide 1, increase the font size of the slide title by selecting the text box and clicking the Increase Font Size button twice.
2. In slide 2, to the right of the main text, without changing the slide layout, add the PowerPoint clip-art image "Anxiety Stress" (a cartoon character sitting at a computer) from the Cartoons category. (If your copy of PowerPoint doesn't have this clip-art image or the ones that follow, use another one of your choice.) *Hint*: Use the Insert Clip Art button on the Standard toolbar, then resize and move the graphic image so that it fits neatly to the right of the text.
3. In slide 3, replace the clip-art placeholder with the "Information Newspaper" image from the Cartoons category.
4. In slide 4 add a clip-art image to the right of the main text. From the Communication category, use "Telephone Communication."

5. In slide 5 insert the picture artist.wmf if you can find it on your disk. *Hint*: If your computer system has Microsoft Office installed on it, you can find the file by clicking the Start button in the lower-left corner of your screen, clicking Find, clicking Files or Folders, and then typing "artist.wmf" and having the Find facility look in your hard disk for the file. When you find the file, note the directory it is in and close Find File. Then, when you insert the picture in PowerPoint, go back to that directory to select the file. If you can't find the file, use some other clip-art image that you think is appropriate.

6. Add a slide 6 with a "Graph" layout. Create a title with the text "Typical Costs of Preparing a Document." Select the graph type by double-clicking the graph placeholder, then clicking the down arrow to the right of the Chart Type button and clicking the line graph icon (fourth row, first column). Create a line graph with the following information:
   a. Column labels (columns A through I, respectively): 0, 5, 10, 15, 20, 25, 30, 35, 40.
   b. First row data (cells A1 through I1, respectively): 0, 300, 250, 200, 175, 150, 125, 125, 125.
   c. Delete other rows and columns.
   d. Y-axis title (change to vertical orientation): "Cost per page"
   e. X-axis title: "Number of pages"
   f. Delete the legend. *Hint:* Click it, then press the Delete key.
7. Use Slide Show to review the entire presentation.
8. Save the file, then print the slides in black and white as three slides per page.
9. Close the file.

4. Presentation on Past Employment or Service Prepare a presentation dealing with one of your past employment or volunteer service experiences. Employment could include any paid or unpaid work you have done. Service could include work for your own family or volunteer work in your community, church, club, or school. In creating your presentation, do the following:
1. Select an appropriate design template.
2. Create a title slide with the title "My Work as a..." or "Employment in the... Industry." Use your name as the subtitle.
3. Include at least four slides. Slide topics might be "My Duties," "Work Conditions," "Working with Other Employees," "My Boss," "How to Be More Efficient," "Pay and Benefits," "Holidays and Other Days Off," and "Recommendations for Future Employees."
4. Include at least one graph. For example, you could create a pie chart showing the percent of time spent daily on each type of duty, a bar graph showing your hourly pay for each quarterly or annual time period, or a bar graph showing hourly pay of your job compared with the same job at other places of employment. If you don't have real numbers available, make up reasonable numbers.
5. Include clip-art or other graphic images on at least three slides.
6. Save your presentation using the filename Case 4 - My Job. If you get an error message that your Student Disk is full, then save the file to a new, blank disk.
7. Print your presentation slides, making sure they are legible in black and white.
8. Close the file.

Presenting a Slide Show

Annual Report of Inca Imports International

OBJECTIVES

In this tutorial you will learn to:

▪ Change the slide color scheme and background shading style

▪ Modify the color and character of bullets

▪ Add a logo to the Slide Master

▪ Insert slides from another slide presentation

▪ Add a footer to the bottom of each slide

▪ Apply transitions and builds to slides

▪ Annotate slides during a slide show

▪ Use the PowerPoint Viewer

▪ Create 35mm slides and overhead transparencies

CASE

Report to Investors

A year after receiving venture capital from Commercial Financial Bank of Southern California, Patricia Cuevas needs to present her first annual report on Inca Imports International's progress. She will make two presentations: one to the company's board of directors and one to the company stockholders. Patricia decides that she can create one slide show for both audiences and that she should include slides about Inca Imports' successful marketing campaign. Patricia has asked you to help her prepare the presentation.

In this tutorial, you will create a title slide, gather previously created slides, and arrange and order the slides to create her slide show.

SESSION

4.1

In this session, you'll learn how to use the Slide Master to make changes that affect the overall appearance of your presentation. By using the Slide Master you will choose the slide color scheme, change the bullet and font styles, and add a logo to each slide in the presentation.

DESIGN
window

PREPARING FOR A PRESENTATION MEETING

- Prepare an agenda. Include date, time, place, topics for discussion, names of presenters, and, if it's a small meeting, the attendees. List any materials needed for the meeting.
- Prepare your presentation. Request help from others, as necessary, and then follow up.
- Have a backup copy of your presentation to use in case you run into any equipment failures.
- Check the physical arrangements, including size of the room, chairs, tables, podium, and thermostat setting.
- Check the needed equipment, including the microphone, chalkboard or white board with chalk or markers, computer with projection system (if you're giving an on-screen presentation), slide projector, overhead projector, VCR, and TV (if you're using video).
- Prepare other items, as needed, including handouts, beverages, refreshments, pads, pencils, name cards, and reference materials.

Planning the Presentation

Before starting PowerPoint, Patricia identifies the purpose of and audience for her presentation.

- **Purpose of the presentation:** To present an overview of the progress that Inca Imports has made during the past year

- **Type of presentation:** General presentation

- **Audience for the presentation:** Inca's board of directors; stockholders of Inca Imports at their annual meeting

- **Audience needs:** A quick overview of Inca's performance over the past year

- **Location of the presentation:** Small boardroom for the board of directors; large conference room at the meeting site for the stockholders

- **Format:** Oral presentation; on-screen slide show for the board of directors; 35mm slide show for the stockholders; both presentations to consist of five to seven slides

Opening a Blank Presentation

Because you are going to combine previously created slides with new slides, you will open a blank presentation instead of using the AutoContent Wizard. You will begin by opening a blank presentation and creating a title slide.

To open a blank presentation:

1. Start PowerPoint, and from the PowerPoint startup dialog box, click **Blank Presentation**, then click the **OK** button. The New Slide dialog box opens with the AutoLayout selections.

   TROUBLE? If you've already started PowerPoint, close all other presentations and click the New button on the Standard toolbar.

2. Make sure the Title Slide layout is selected, then click the **OK** button. The placeholders for a title slide appear on the screen in Slide View.

3. If the presentation window is not maximized, click the **Maximize** button of the presentation window.

4. Click the title placeholder and type **Annual Report**.

5. Click the subtitle placeholder and type **Inca Imports International**.

6. Click anywhere outside of any text boxes to deselect them. Your screen should look like Figure 4-1.

Figure 4-1 ◀
Title slide of
blank
presentation

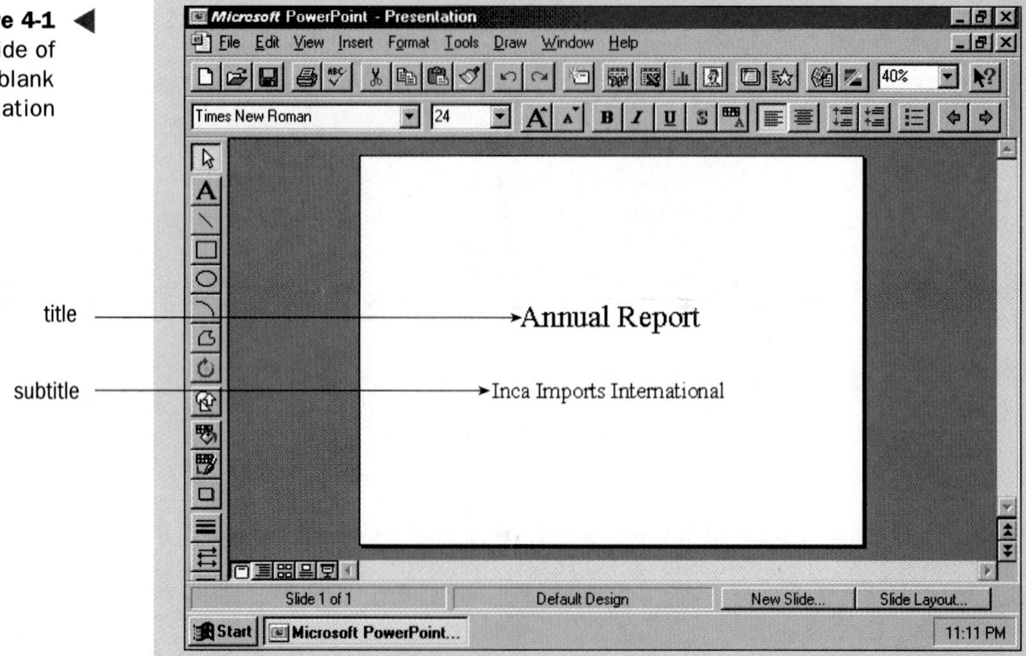

title

subtitle

You have now created the title slide of the annual report.

Using the Slide Master

When you open a new blank presentation, the default background is white with no design. Patricia wants you to select a **color scheme**, that is, an overall color design for the slides in her presentation. When you create a blank presentation, you should choose either a design template or a color scheme. You will apply the color scheme to the Slide Master. The **Slide Master** is a slide that contains text and graphics that appear on all the slides (except the title slide) in the presentation and controls the format and color of the text and background on all slides. Changes made to the master are reflected on all the slides in the presentation, except for the title slide. You can also create a Master for outlines, handouts, and speaker's notes.

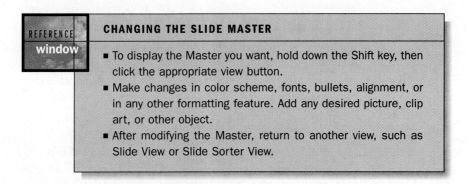

REFERENCE
window

CHANGING THE SLIDE MASTER

- To display the Master you want, hold down the Shift key, then click the appropriate view button.
- Make changes in color scheme, fonts, bullets, alignment, or in any other formatting feature. Add any desired picture, clip art, or other object.
- After modifying the Master, return to another view, such as Slide View or Slide Sorter View.

Let's display the Slide Master.

To display the Slide Master:

1. Hold down the **Shift** key and position the pointer over the **Slide View** button ▣. The ToolTip now reads Slide Master. See Figure 4-2.

Figure 4-2
Slide Master
ToolTip

ToolTip when you
press Shift

2. With the Shift key still pressed, click the **Slide View** button ▣. Alternatively, you could click **View**, click **Master**, then click **Slide Master**. The Slide Master appears in the presentation window. See Figure 4-3.

Figure 4-3
Slide Master in
presentation
window

blank Slide Master

slide indicator

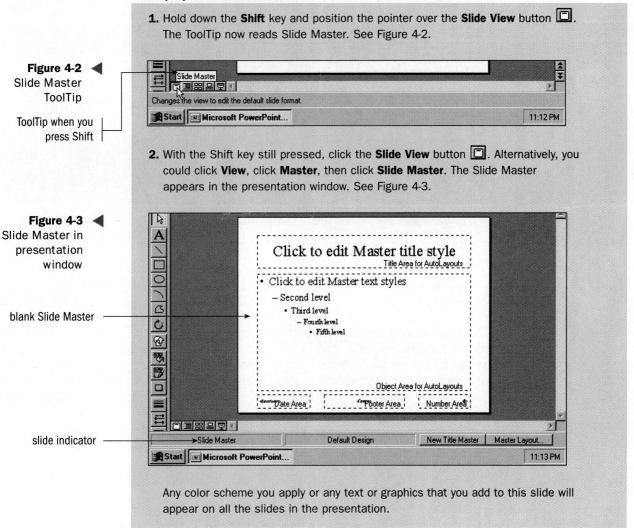

Any color scheme you apply or any text or graphics that you add to this slide will appear on all the slides in the presentation.

With the Slide Master in the PowerPoint presentation window, you are now ready to change the color scheme.

Changing the Slide Color Scheme

You can make changes to individual slides without using the Slide Master, but certain changes—like adding text, changing the style of bullets, or inserting a logo—should be made on the Slide Master to take effect on all the slides and promote overall consistency in the presentation. Let's change the color scheme of the slides now.

To change the slide color scheme:

1. Click **Format**, then click **Slide Color Scheme**. The Color Scheme dialog box opens. See Figure 4-4. If necessary, click the **Standard** tab in the dialog box.

Figure 4-4 ◄
Color Scheme
dialog box

select this
color scheme

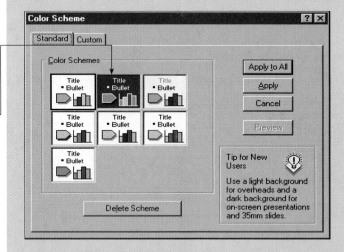

Patricia wants you to select a dark background color because she will deliver her presentation using slides rather than overheads.

2. Click the color scheme icon with the blue background.

3. Click the **Apply to All** button. You could also click the Apply button. Because you are working on the Slide Master, any change to this slide will apply to all slides.

The background color is now blue, the title text is yellow, and the main text is white, which is an attractive and readable color scheme. You can change the color scheme for the entire presentation without using the Slide Master, but other changes, such as modifying bullets and fonts, take effect on all the slides only if you use the Slide Master. Therefore, it's a good idea to always use the Slide Master when you are making design decisions so that all your slides will be consistent.

Although the background color you've selected is appropriate and attractive, you can change the background from solid blue to a shaded blue to improve its appearance. Let's make this change now.

To change the solid background color to a shaded style:

1. Click **Format**, then click **Custom Background**. The Custom Background dialog box opens. See Figure 4-5.

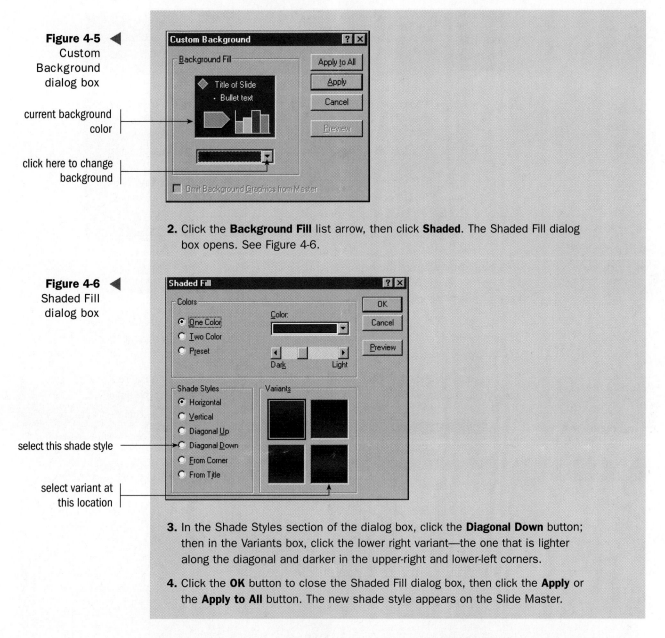

Figure 4-5
Custom
Background
dialog box

current background
color

click here to change
background

Figure 4-6
Shaded Fill
dialog box

select this shade style

select variant at
this location

2. Click the **Background Fill** list arrow, then click **Shaded**. The Shaded Fill dialog box opens. See Figure 4-6.

3. In the Shade Styles section of the dialog box, click the **Diagonal Down** button; then in the Variants box, click the lower right variant—the one that is lighter along the diagonal and darker in the upper-right and lower-left corners.

4. Click the **OK** button to close the Shaded Fill dialog box, then click the **Apply** or the **Apply to All** button. The new shade style appears on the Slide Master.

You can also change the background color from the Custom Background dialog box. However, by using a preset color scheme from the Slide Color Scheme dialog box, you will always get readable background and font colors in your presentations.

Modifying the Bullets and Font on the Slide Master

Patricia likes the color scheme you have chosen, except that she would like the bullets to be a different color from the main text. She also wants you to change the character, or style, used for the bullets. To change the bullets for all the slides in the presentation, you will again modify the Slide Master.

CHANGING BULLETS

- If you want the change in bullets to affect all slides in the presentation, display the Slide Master by holding down the Shift key and then clicking the Slide View button.
- Click anywhere within the text of the bulleted item.
- Click Format, then click Bullet to display the Bullet dialog box.
- To change the font (so you can select a new bullet character), select a font using the Bullets From list, then click the desired character.
- To change the color, use the Special Color palette and click the desired color tile.
- Click the OK button.

Let's first change the bullet character and color.

To change the character and color of the bullets:

1. With the Slide Master still in the presentation window, click anywhere in the phrase "Click to edit Master text styles." Now you're ready to change the bullet style and color.

2. Click **Format**, then click **Bullet** to open the Bullet dialog box. See Figure 4-7. The current selection of symbols appears in the grid in the middle of the dialog box.

Figure 4-7 ◄
Bullet dialog box

click to change font

current bullet character

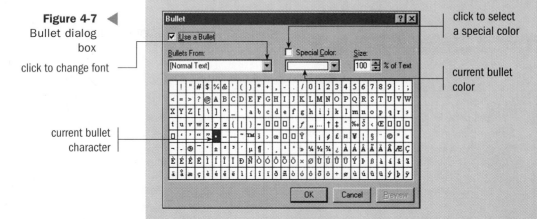

click to select a special color

current bullet color

3. Click the **Bullets From** list arrow, then scroll down and click **Wingdings** or some other font that contains a variety of symbols.

   TROUBLE? If your system doesn't have a symbols font (such as Wingdings, Symbols, Dingbats, or Monotype Sort) available in the Bullets From list, skip to the next set of steps.

4. Click the symbol for a small diamond or for some other symbol that appears in your font. For this presentation, select a simple bullet, like a diamond, square, or circle, that is appropriate for a presentation to stockholders rather than an informal bullet, like a smiling face or a pointing hand. When you click the shapes, the size of the selected shape doubles so you can see it more clearly.

   Next, let's change the bullet color.

5. Click the **Special Color** checkbox. This tells PowerPoint that you want the bullets in your presentation to be a different color from the text color.

6. Click the **Special Color** list arrow to open the Special Color palette, and click the yellow tile. You have now selected a new bullet character and color. See Figure 4-8.

Figure 4-8 ◀
Completed
Bullet dialog
box

new font

new bullet character

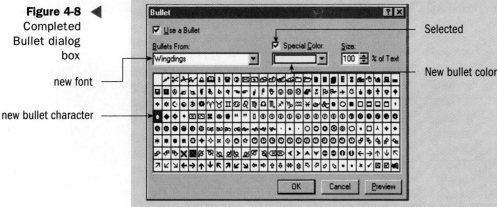

Selected

New bullet color

7. Click the **OK** button on the Bullet dialog box. The dialog box closes, and the first bulleted item on the Slide Master is a yellow diamond (or whatever shape you chose.)

Having changed the color and style of the bullet, you will now change the font of the title on the Slide Master to Arial. Let's make that change now.

To change the title font:

1. On the Slide Master, click the text box labeled "Click to edit Master title style."

2. Click the **Font Face** list arrow on the Formatting toolbar, scroll the font list until "Arial" appears, then click **Arial**.

TROUBLE? If your computer system doesn't have Arial, then use another sans serif font, such as Univers, Avant Garde, or Humanist.

3. Click outside the slide to deselect the text box.

If you had chosen a design template, the color scheme, background, font, font style, and font sizes would have been chosen for you. Instead, you made these decisions by using the Slide Master.

Adding a Logo to the Slide Master

Finally, Patricia wants to add the Inca Imports International logo to the Slide Master, so it will appear on every slide in the presentation. To add a picture to the Slide Master, you follow the same procedure as adding a picture to a regular slide.

To add a picture to a Slide Master:

1. Click **Insert**, then click **Picture** to open the Insert Picture dialog box.

2. If it's not there already, insert the Student Disk into drive A or B, make that disk drive the current drive, and make sure **Tutorial.04** folder appears in the Look in text box of the Insert Picture dialog box. Open the Tutorial.04 folder.

3. Click **Incalogo** to select the logo, then click the **OK** button to insert the logo into the middle of the Slide Master. Because the logo will be on all the slides, Patricia wants you to make it smaller and move it to the upper-left corner of the slide.

4. Drag the logo on top of the box labeled "Title Area for AutoLayout" so its upper-left corner is located at or near the upper-left corner of the title text box.

5. Drag the lower-right resize handle up and to the left so that the height of the image is the same size as the text box. See Figure 4-9.

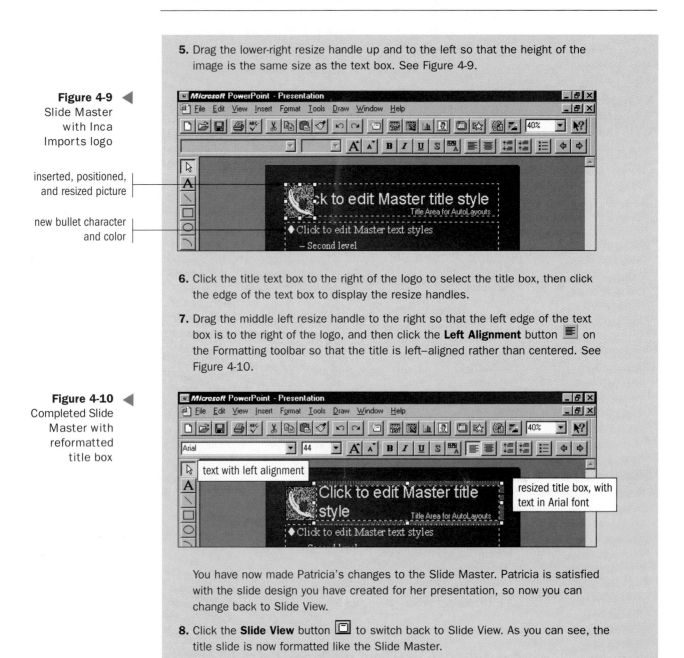

Figure 4-9 ◀
Slide Master
with Inca
Imports logo

inserted, positioned, and resized picture

new bullet character and color

6. Click the title text box to the right of the logo to select the title box, then click the edge of the text box to display the resize handles.

7. Drag the middle left resize handle to the right so that the left edge of the text box is to the right of the logo, and then click the **Left Alignment** button 📊 on the Formatting toolbar so that the title is left–aligned rather than centered. See Figure 4-10.

Figure 4-10 ◀
Completed Slide
Master with
reformatted
title box

text with left alignment

resized title box, with text in Arial font

You have now made Patricia's changes to the Slide Master. Patricia is satisfied with the slide design you have created for her presentation, so now you can change back to Slide View.

8. Click the **Slide View** button 🔲 to switch back to Slide View. As you can see, the title slide is now formatted like the Slide Master.

You have worked for fifteen minutes or so on the presentation, so you should save your work to this point. In addition, you can enter information (called **properties**) about the slide presentation file into the Presentation Properties dialog box.

To save the slide presentation:

1. Click **File**, then click **Properties** on the Menu bar. The Presentation Properties dialog box opens. Make sure the Summary tab is in the foreground.

2. Leave the title as Annual Report, and then by clicking in each box or pressing the **Tab** key to move to each box, change the Subject to **Report to Board of Directors and Stockholders**, the Author to **Patricia Cuevas**, the Company to **Inca Imports International**, the Keywords to **Annual Report**, and leave the other text boxes blank. See Figure 4-11.

Figure 4-11
Presentation
Properties
dialog box

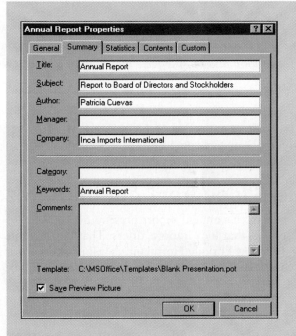

3. Click the **OK** button to close the Presentation Properties dialog box.

4. Click the **Save** button 🖫 on the Formatting toolbar, then save the presentation to the Tutorial.04 folder on your Student Disk using the filename Annual Report. PowerPoint saves the presentation to the disk.

Quick Check

[1] List the major items that you should include in your preparation for a presentation meeting.

[2] Define or describe the following terms:
a. background shade style
b. variant (of a background shade style)

[3] Describe the purpose of the Slide Master and when you would use it.

[4] What is an advantage for creating a slide show beginning with a blank slide presentation rather than using the AutoContent Wizard?

[5] How would you do the following?
a. display the Slide Master
b. change the color scheme of a slide
c. change the shading (and variant) of the background color
d. modify a bullet character and color

[6] How do you add a picture to a Slide Master?

This concludes Session 4.1. You can exit PowerPoint or continue to the next session.

SESSION

4.2

In this session, you'll learn how to insert slides from an existing presentation into your presentation and how to add a footer to the bottom of each slide. You'll also learn how to add transition and build effects and how to annotate the slide show.

If you exited PowerPoint at the end of the previous session, start the program again, open the presentation file Annual Report from your Student Disk, and select Slide View. If you are continuing from the previous session, select Slide View.

Inserting Slides from Another Presentation

Patricia's first task in this annual report presentation is to review with her audience the products and services that Inca Imports offers. That information, however, already exists in the presentation that Enrique Hoffmann developed earlier for the marketing division. Patricia asks you to insert slides from Enrique's presentation into the current one.

REFERENCE
window

INSERTING SLIDES FROM AN EXISTING PRESENTATION

- Go to Slide View, then display the slide after which you want to insert the existing presentation slides.
- Click Insert, then click Slides from File.
- Select the disk and filename that contains the existing presentation, then click the Insert button.

Let's insert slides from an existing presentation now.

To insert slides from an existing file:

  1. With the title slide of the annual report still in the presentation window in Slide View, click **Insert**, then click **Slides from File**. PowerPoint displays the Insert File dialog box. When you insert slides from another presentation, you must insert the entire file, then delete the slides you don't want.

  2. With the Look in box set to the Tutorial.04 folder, click **Products** from the list of filenames, then click the **Insert** button to insert the slides from the existing presentation into the current presentation.

Slide 2 of Enrique's presentation appears in the presentation window. This is the title slide from the earlier presentation. You can delete this slide.

To delete a slide:

  1. Click **Edit** then click **Delete Slide** to delete the current slide. Then go to the new slide 2, which is titled "Providing Quality Produce." See Figure 4-12. The slide has the color scheme of the current slide presentation, not of the original presentation from which it came.

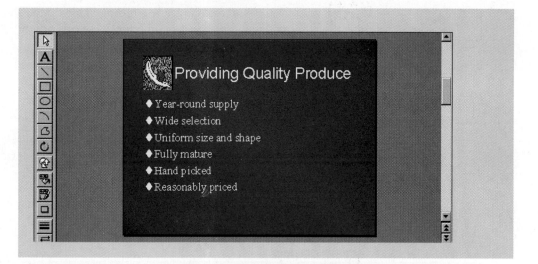

Figure 4-12 ◀
New slide 2
with updated
design

Now the slides from Enrique's presentation are formatted and changed for Patricia's presentation.

Completing the Slide Presentation

Next Patricia wants you to change the order of the slides to meet the needs of her presentation, delete unwanted slides, and add new slides as needed. To sort the slides, you'll use Slide Sorter View. You can also change the order of slides in Outline View. Let's sort the slides now.

To change the order of the slides:

1. Click the **Slide Sorter View** button 🔡 at the bottom of the presentation window. PowerPoint displays the slides of the presentation and the Slide Sorter toolbar appears below the Standard toolbar. Patricia wants to move slide 3, "Meeting Your Needs," so that it becomes slide 2.

2. Click on and drag slide 3 to the left, and watch as a vertical line follows the pointer. Release the mouse button when the vertical line is between slides 1 and 2. Patricia decides that she wants you to delete slide 4, "Reducing Time to Market."

3. Click slide 4 to make it the current slide, then press the **Delete** key to delete the slide from the presentation. See Figure 4-13.

Figure 4-13 ◀
Slide Sorter
View after
moving a slide
and deleting a
slide

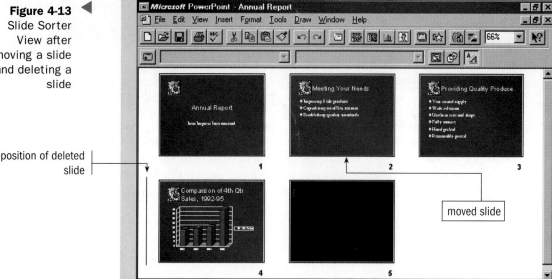

position of deleted
slide

moved slide

Next, Patricia wants you to change the wording in the title of slide 2. You can't change text in Slide Sorter View. You must be in Slide View or Outline View to edit slide text. Let's change the title of the slide now.

To edit slide text:

1. Click slide 2, then click the **Slide View** button ⬚ at the bottom of the presentation window. PowerPoint displays slide 2 in the presentation window.

2. Using methods you've learned previously, change the title from "Meeting Your Needs" to "Meeting Customer Needs." Then deselect the title text box.

Now Patricia wants you to add a slide to the presentation that summarizes the performance of her company.

To add new slides:

1. From within Slide View, move to slide 4 of the presentation.

2. Click the **Insert New Slide** button ⬚ on the Standard toolbar to insert a new slide into the presentation and open the New Slide dialog box. You could also have clicked the New Slide button at the bottom of the presentation window.

3. Click the layout titled "Bulleted List," then click the **OK** button.

4. Click the title placeholder and type **Inca's Solid Performance**.

5. Click the main text (bulleted list) text box and type three bulleted items: **Improved products and services**, **Implemented new marketing plan**, and **Increased profitability**.

6. Click outside the text boxes to see the completed slide. See Figure 4-14.

Figure 4-14 ◀
Completed new slide 5

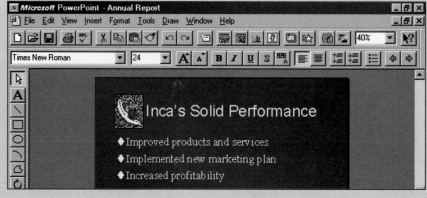

That completes the new slide 5.

Adding a Footer

Patricia wants the company name to appear at the bottom of every slide in her presentation. She knows that rather than add the text to each slide individually, she can use a footer. A **footer** is text near the bottom of a slide that contains information such as the date and time the presentation was created, the slide number, the company name, or the title of the presentation.

Because the title slide already displays the company name, Patricia does not want the footer to appear at the bottom of the title slide.

To add a footer to the presentation:

1. Click **View**, then click **Header and Footer** on the Menu bar. The Header and Footer dialog box opens. If necessary, click the Slide tab to bring it forward. See Figure 4-15.

Figure 4-15 ◀
Header and
Footer dialog
box

deselect this ⟶

keep deselected ⟶

keep selected ⟶

text box for footer ⟶

select this ⟶

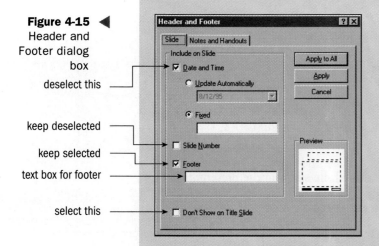

Because Patricia doesn't want the date and time or slide number to appear in the footer, you should turn off those options.

2. If necessary, click the **Date and Time** check box and click the **Slide Number** check box so that neither is selected.

3. If necessary, click the **Footer** check box so that it is selected, and in the text box beneath it, type **Inca Imports International**.

4. Click the **Don't Show on Title Slide** check box to hide the footer on the title slide. See Figure 4-16.

Figure 4-16 ◀
Completed
Header and
Footer
dialog box

text of footer ⟶

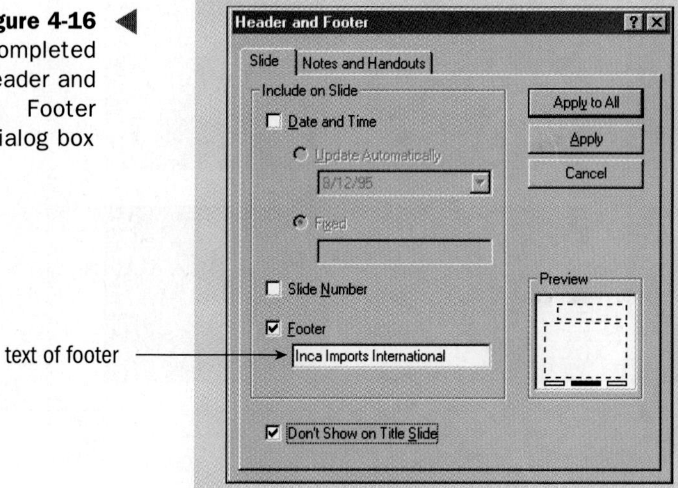

5. Click the **Apply to All** button. The dialog box closes, and the footer appears at the bottom of the current slide.

6. Select slide 1. Notice that the footer does not appear on the title slide.

Now Patricia wants you to add special effects to improve the interest of the slide show.

Adding Transition Effects

The first special effect that Patricia wants you to add is called a transition effect. A **transition effect** is a method of moving one slide off the screen and bringing another slide onto the screen during a slide show. You must be in Slide Sorter View to add transitions.

REFERENCE window	**ADDING TRANSITION EFFECTS**
	■ Get into Slide Sorter View and select the slide or slides to which you want to add a transition effect.
	■ Click the Slide Transition Effects list arrow on the Formatting toolbar to display a list of transition effects.
	■ Click the desired transition effect.

Let's add a transition to all the slides in the presentation.

To add a transition effect:

1. Click the **Slide Sorter View** button 🔲 at the bottom of the presentation window to change to Slide Sorter View.

2. Click **Edit** then click **Select All** to select all the slides in the presentation. Now when you apply a slide transition, all the slides will have that transition. Currently, the Formatting toolbar shows "No Transition" in the Slide Transition Effects box. See Figure 4-17.

Figure 4-17 ◀
All six slides
selected

current transition
effect

presentation window
with selected slides

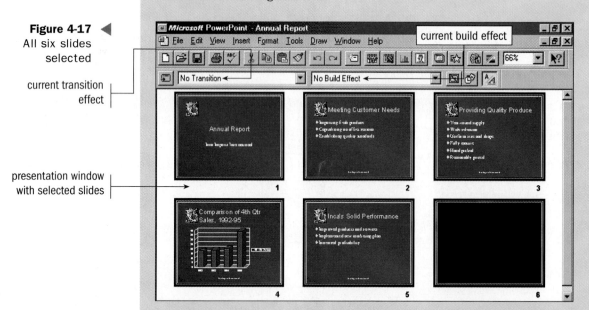

3. Click the **Slide Transition Effects** list arrow on the Slide Sorter toolbar to display the list of transitions.

4. Scroll through the list until **Dissolve** appears, then click that transition. If you watched carefully, you saw PowerPoint demonstrate the dissolve transition on the first slide.

5. Click anywhere outside of a slide to deselect the slides. A transition icon appears below the lower-left corner of each slide. See Figure 4-18.

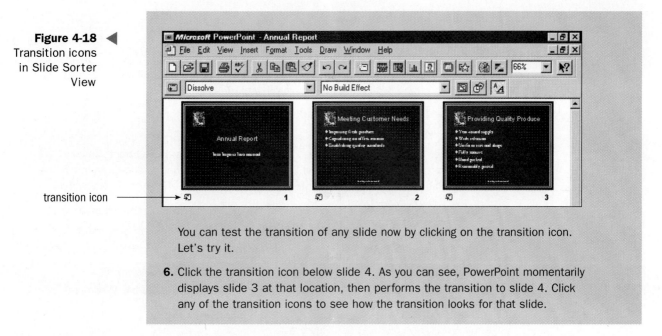

Figure 4-18 ◄
Transition icons
in Slide Sorter
View

transition icon ⟶

You can test the transition of any slide now by clicking on the transition icon. Let's try it.

6. Click the transition icon below slide 4. As you can see, PowerPoint momentarily displays slide 3 at that location, then performs the transition to slide 4. Click any of the transition icons to see how the transition looks for that slide.

You have now added transitions to the slides. You added the same transition to all six slides, but if you wanted, you could have selected one slide at a time and created a unique transition for only that slide.

Adding Build Effects

Having added transitions to the slides, you are ready to add another special effect: builds. A **build** (also known as a **progressive disclosure**) is a feature that allows you to progressively display individual bulleted items, one item at a time. For example, if a slide has several bulleted items, you can add a build to the slide so that when you first display the slide in your slide show, the slide title appears, but none of the bulleted items appear. Then when you press the spacebar or click the left mouse button, the first bulleted item appears. When you press the spacebar or click the left mouse button again, the second bulleted item appears, and so on. You can also tell PowerPoint to dim the previous item as a new one is added. The advantage of builds is that you can focus your audience's attention on one item at a time, without the distractions of other items on the screen. You must be in Slide Sorter View to add builds.

REFERENCE
window

ADDING A BUILD EFFECT

- In Slide Sorter View, select the slide or slides to which you want to add a build effect.
- Click the Text Build Effects list arrow on the Formatting toolbar to display a list of transition effects.
- Click the desired build effect.
- To dim previous points in the build, click Tools, click Build Slide Text, then click Other; click the After Build Step list arrow, click the tile of the desired color, then click the OK button.

Let's add a build effect now.

To add a build effect:

1. Click slide 2, then press and hold down the **Shift** key, and click slides 3 and 5 to select the three slides that have bulleted lists. Release the Shift key.

2. Click the **Text Build Effects** list arrow on the Slide Sorter toolbar to display the list of builds.

3. Scroll down and click **Wipe Right**. This specifies the type of build effect you want. In this case, the text in each bulleted item appears on the screen from left to right as if someone wiped it onto the screen.

   Now Patricia wants you to tell PowerPoint to dim the old bulleted item when a new item is displayed. This is called "dimming previous points."

4. Click **Tools**, click **Build Slide Text**, then click **Other** on the Menu bar to open the Animation Settings dialog box.

5. Click the **After Build Step** list arrow. A color grid appears below the box that represents the color of the dimmed item. Let's change that color to gray.

6. Click the gray color tile. See Figure 4-19.

Figure 4-19 ◀
Animation Settings dialog box

build effect ────▶

new dim color ───

Animation Settings   `? X`

Build Options
By 1st Level Paragraphs   ▼   OK
☐ In reverse order   Cancel
☐ Start when previous build ends

Effects
Wipe Right   ▼   Build this object:
    By Paragraph   ▼   ▼
[No Sound]   ▼   After Build Step:
                                 →   ▼

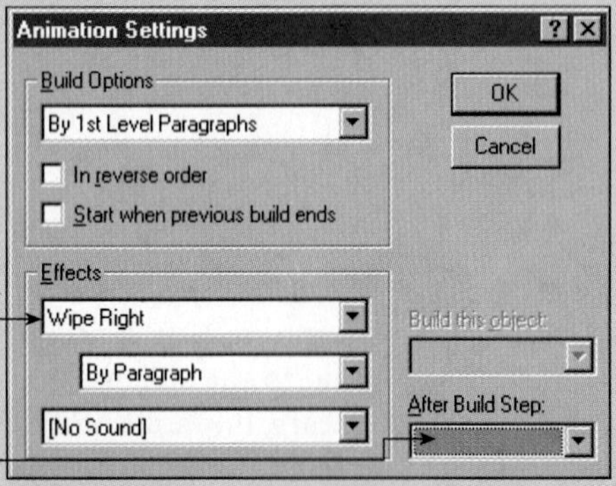

7. Click the **OK** button to add build effect icons below slides 2, 3, and 5, the three slides to which you have added build effects. See Figure 4-20.

Figure 4-20 ◀
Slides with build effect icons

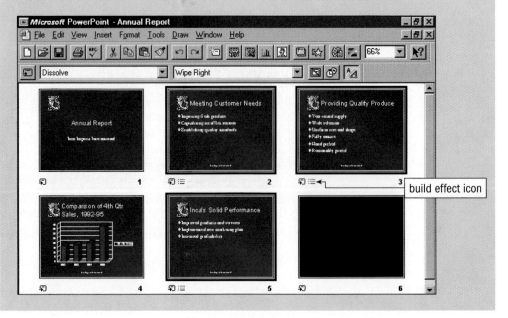

build effect icon

8. Click anywhere outside the slides to deselect them. You have now added build effects to the appropriate slides. You could have added different build effects to each slide by selecting each slide individually and then completing Steps 2 through 7.

You can't see a build while in Slide Sorter View; you must be in Slide Show View. Let's run the completed slide show to view our special effects—the transitions and builds.

Running the Slide Show

Now that you have completed Patricia's slide show, she is ready to view it. Let's view the presentation using the Slide Show View.

To view the completed presentation:

1. Click slide 1 in Slide Sorter View so that your presentation will begin with slide 1.

2. Click the **Slide Show** button 🖳 at the bottom of the presentation window to begin the slide presentation. The title slide, "Annual Report," appears on the screen.

3. Press the **spacebar** to advance to the next slide. (You can also use the arrow keys, the page up and page down keys, or the mouse button.) Notice that when you advance to the next slide, it "dissolves" onto the screen because of the transition effect. Only the title and footer of slide 2, "Meeting Customer Needs," appear on the screen because this is a build slide, which will disclose the bulleted items one at a time as you proceed.

4. Press the **spacebar** to display the first bulleted item, "Importing fresh produce."

5. Press the **spacebar** to display the second bulleted item and dim the first one. See Figure 4-21.

Figure 4-21 ◀
Build effect with
previous item
dimmed

dimmed item ——

current item ——

6. Continue through the slide show, pressing the spacebar to advance from one slide to the next or, within a build slide, from one item to the next. When you get to the last slide, the one with the black background, stop there.

TROUBLE? If you advanced past the last slide, PowerPoint returned you to the Slide Sorter View. Just click the Slide Show button again, then press the End key to return to the last slide.

At this point, Patricia decides that she wants to look at the "Inca's Solid Performance" slide again.

7. Press ← once to move the presentation backward to the previous slide. Notice that when you go back to the previous slide, the last bulleted item appears in the normal color, and all other bulleted items are dimmed. If you wanted to go backward through the build effect, you could press ← multiple times.

8. Press the **Escape** key to return to Slide Sorter View.

Patricia is pleased with your results. You should now save the final version of her slide show to your Student Disk.

To save the slide show:

1. Click the **Save** button ⊞ on the Standard toolbar to save the presentation file using the default filename "Annual Report."

Patricia will rehearse her slide show next.

Annotating Slides During a Slide Show

While Patricia is rehearsing her slide presentation, and during the actual presentation to the stockholders, she will annotate certain slides to draw attention to important points. To **annotate** a slide in PowerPoint means to make temporary freehand marks on the slide during a slide presentation. The annotations are temporary and will not be saved to the presentation.

REFERENCE
window

ANNOTATING A SLIDE

- While showing a slide show in Slide Show View, advance to the slide you wish to annotate.
- Click the Slide Show Options icon in the lower-left corner of the screen and click Pen.
- Use the pencil pointer to make temporary marks on the slide.

Let's annotate the presentation now.

To annotate a slide:

1. From Slide Sorter View, click slide 3 to select it.

2. Click the **Slide Show** button 🖵. Slide 3 appears in Slide Show View.

3. Press the **spacebar** six times to see the last bulleted item, "Reasonably priced."

4. Move the mouse to display the pointer on the screen and to display the Slide Show Options icon in the lower-left corner of the screen. See Figure 4-22.

Figure 4-22 ◀
Slide 3 of
Slide Show

Slide Show
Options icon

moved pointer

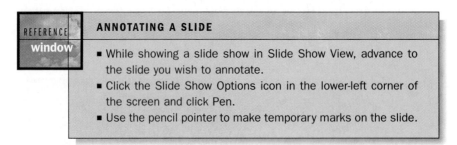
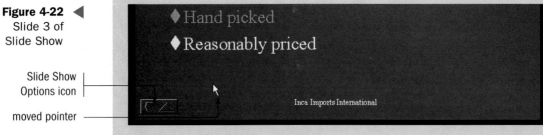

◆ Hand picked
◆ Reasonably priced

Inca Imports International

Patricia wants to emphasize that Inca produce is reasonably priced, neither the highest nor the lowest in the industry.

5. Click the **Slide Show Options** icon in the lower-left corner of the screen. The options list appears above the icon.

6. Click **Pen**. The options list disappears and the pointer becomes ✎.

7. Position ✎ under the "R" in "Reasonably," then hold down the left mouse button while you drag the pointer to underline that word. Then release the mouse button. See Figure 4-23. Patricia rehearses what she will say to emphasize the meaning of "reasonably priced." If you want to add a straight line, hold down the Shift key when you drag the pointer.

Figure 4-23 ◀
Slide 3 with annotation

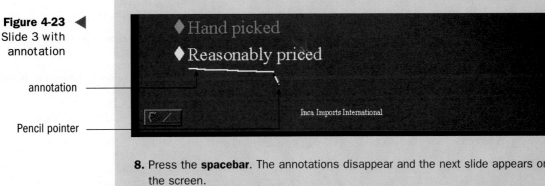

annotation ——————

Pencil pointer ——————

8. Press the **spacebar**. The annotations disappear and the next slide appears on the screen.

9. Press the **Escape** key to quit the slide show.

After rehearsing her presentation several times, Patricia feels confident about making the presentation to the stockholders.

DESIGN
window

TIPS ON ELECTRONIC PRESENTATIONS

- Don't feel that you have to include transitions and builds in your slides. Transitions and builds can distract your audience from the message of the presentation.
- If you include transitions, use only one type of transition for all the slides.
- If you include builds, use only one type of builds for all the build slides.
- If you have a tendency to get nervous during a presentation, avoid using the mouse to advance the slides and to make annotations. The audience can see a jittery mouse pointer on the screen. Use the spacebar to advance slides.
- Avoid excessive annotations on slides. Annotations can look sloppy if done to excess.

Quick Check

1. Define the following terms:
   a. footer
   b. transition effect
   c. build effect
   d. annotation (on a slide)

2. How would you do the following?
   a. insert slides from an existing presentation into the current presentation
   b. add a transition effect to a slide
   c. add a build effect to a slide

3. Why would you want to add a footer to a slide? How would you do it?

4. List one advantage and one disadvantage of adding transition effects to the slides in a presentation.

5. List one advantage and one disadvantage of adding build effects with dimming of previous points to a slide containing bulleted items.

6. How do you go back to the previous slide or bulleted point in Slide Show View?

This concludes Session 4.2. You can exit PowerPoint or continue to the next session.

SESSION

4.3

In this session, you'll learn how to run your presentation on a computer that doesn't have PowerPoint installed. You'll also learn how to create 35mm slides and overhead transparencies.

If you exited PowerPoint at the end of the previous session, start the program again, then open the presentation file "Annual Report" from your Student Disk.

Using the PowerPoint Viewer

You could run all your presentations from the PowerPoint program, but what if you want to give a presentation on a computer that doesn't have PowerPoint installed? In that case, you could use the PowerPoint Viewer. The **PowerPoint Viewer** is a separate program that you can use to show your presentation on any Windows 95 or Windows NT computer. The Microsoft PowerPoint license allows you to create a Viewer disk and to install the Viewer program on other computers without additional charge.

Patricia wants you to get Angelena Cristenas's opinion on her presentation, but Angelena doesn't have PowerPoint on her computer. Using the **Pack and Go Wizard**, you can create a Viewer disk that contains the PowerPoint Viewer files and a copy of Patricia's presentation. In a sense, the Pack and Go Wizard makes PowerPoint a portable program.

To create a PowerPoint Viewer disk:

1. If necessary, start PowerPoint and open the presentation file Annual Report. Then remove the Student Disk and place a blank formatted disk in drive A.

   TROUBLE? To complete these steps, you will need a formatted disk that can be used as a Viewer disk. If you are working in a lab or on a network, you should consult your instructor or technical support person to find out if you are allowed to install files on another computer. If you don't have a blank disk or you are not allowed to copy files, skip this section.

2. Click **File** then click **Pack And Go** to open the Pack and Go Wizard dialog box. The Pack and Go Wizard will ask you a series of questions that will give it enough information to create the Viewer disk.

3. Click the **Next** button. The Pack and Go Wizard displays the title slide of the current presentation and allows you to select which presentations you would like to copy onto the Viewer disk. See Figure 4-24.

Figure 4-24 ◀
Pack and Go
Wizard dialog
box

current presentation
file selected

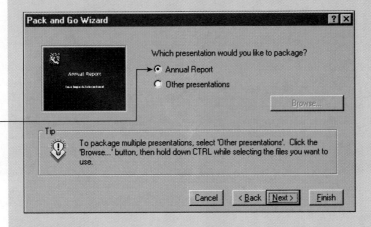

Because you want to show only the current slide show, you should accept the default choice.

4. Click the **Next** button, then on the dialog box, click the drive A or drive B button, depending on which drive contains your blank, formatted disk.

5. Click the **Next** button three times to accept the default answer to each of the remaining Pack and Go Wizard questions.

6. Click the **Finish** button. After a few minutes, PowerPoint copies the Viewer files and the presentation to your disk.

You are now ready to use your "Pack and Go" disk to install the Viewer and presentation files on Angelena's computer.

To copy the Viewer files and run the presentation on another computer:

1. On the other computer, click the **Start** button on the taskbar at the bottom of the Windows desktop. Then click **Run**. The Run dialog box opens.

2. In the Open box, type **a:pngsetup** and click the **OK** button. The Pack and Go Setup dialog box opens. See Figure 4-25.

Figure 4-25 ◀
Pack and Go
Setup window

enter destination
folder name here

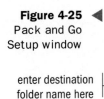
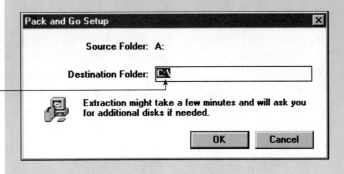

TROUBLE? Because version 7 of the PowerPoint Viewer runs only on Windows 95 or Windows NT, the computer on which you want to give the slide presentation must be running one of those operating systems.

3. In the Destination Folder box, type **c:\viewer** (or the name of the folder where you want the Viewer files to be copied) and click the **OK** button. PowerPoint copies the files from the Viewer disk into the folder you specify and then asks you if you want to run the presentation.

4. If the folder you specified doesn't exist, you will be asked if you want to create it. Click the **OK** button to create the new folder.

5. Click the **Yes** button to run the presentation. Clicking Yes from the Pack and Go Setup is the same as clicking the Slide Show button in the PowerPoint presentation window on your own computer.

6. Press the **spacebar** or click the left mouse button to run through each slide in the presentation, or press the **Escape** key to stop the slide show whenever you want. Remove the Viewer disk from the drive when you are done.

Angelena liked Patricia's presentation. Although she can't change any of the files using the PowerPoint Viewer, she is able to review each one.

Preparing 35mm Slides

Patricia will present the electronic slide show to the board of directors in a suitably equipped conference room at Inca Imports. The conference room at the stockholders meeting, however, does not have the equipment necessary to run an electronic slide show, so Patricia plans to use 35mm slides. Because the presentation to the stockholders is very important, Patricia also makes black-and-white overhead transparencies as a backup to the slides.

Inca Imports International, like most small businesses, lacks the facilities to make 35mm slides or print color output from computer files, but all large U.S. cities have service bureaus that can convert computer files into 35mm slides, provided the files are in the correct format, usually PostScript. You should contact a service bureau near you for details. Check the yellow pages of your telephone book under "Typesetting."

PowerPoint also supports the services of Genigraphics Corporation, a service bureau that handles 35mm slides, color overheads, and posters. With headquarters in Memphis, Tennessee, Genigraphics has facilities in many major cities around the United States. The PowerPoint disks contain the software necessary to prepare and deliver slides to Genigraphics. Patricia therefore decides to have you use Genigraphics to prepare her slides.

Note: In the following procedure, you will prepare the presentation as if you were going to pay for commercial slide preparation, but you won't actually send the presentation file to Genigraphics.

To begin the Genigraphics Wizard for preparing 35mm slides:

1. If necessary, start PowerPoint again and open Annual Report. Make sure that Annual Report is the only presentation open in PowerPoint. Close any other presentations.

2. Click **File** then click **Slide Setup** to open the Slide Setup dialog box. See Figure 4-26.

Figure 4-26
Slide Setup
dialog box

click here to change
slide size

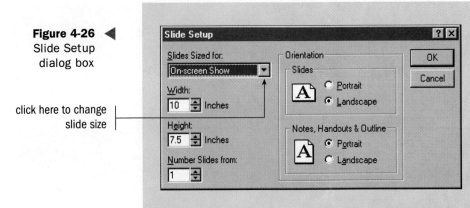

3. Click the **Slides Sized** for list arrow, then click **35mm Slides**. PowerPoint adjusts the width and height of each slide so it is proportioned for 35mm slides. Click the **OK** button.

Now you will output the presentation to a disk file in the Genigraphics format.

4. Click **File** then click **Send to Genigraphics**. The Genigraphics Wizard dialog box opens on the screen. See Figure 4-27. Read the information on the dialog box.

Figure 4-27
Genigraphics
Wizard dialog
box

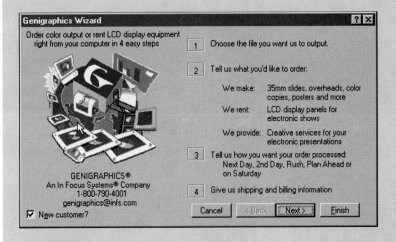

TROUBLE? The Send to Genigraphics option will be available only if your computer has the complete PowerPoint installation. If PowerPoint tells you that it cannot locate or start "GENIWIZ," skip to the next section, "Preparing Overheads."

Now you're ready to use the Genigraphics Wizard to create a file that Genigraphics can use to produce professional-looking slides.

To use the Genigraphics Wizard:

1. Click the **Next** button. The Genigraphics Wizard displays the next dialog box. Make sure the **35mm slides** check box is selected.

2. Click the **Next** button. The file you want to send, Annual Report.ppt should be selected in the dialog box. Click the **Send file on disk** button because you don't want to send the file via modem.

3. Click the **Next** button again. If you get a message that the Genigraphics Wizard needs to save your presentation, click the **Yes** button.

4. Click the **Next** button three times, once to accept the default of plastic mounts, the second time to skip the suggestions to improve the results (none should appear in the dialog box), and the third time to get to the dialog box shown in Figure 4-28.

Figure 4-28 ◀
Genigraphics
Wizard dialog
box

deselect this ────────

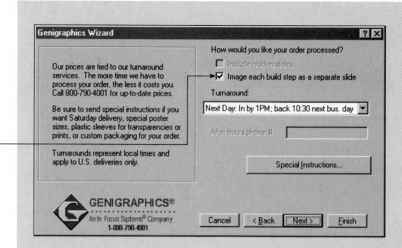

5. Deselect the option **Image each build step as a separate slide**. You want only one slide from Genigraphics for each of the six slides in your presentation.

6. Click the **Next** button and then fill out the dialog box, as shown in Figure 4-29.

Figure 4-29 ◀
Genigraphics
Wizard dialog
box with
completed
information

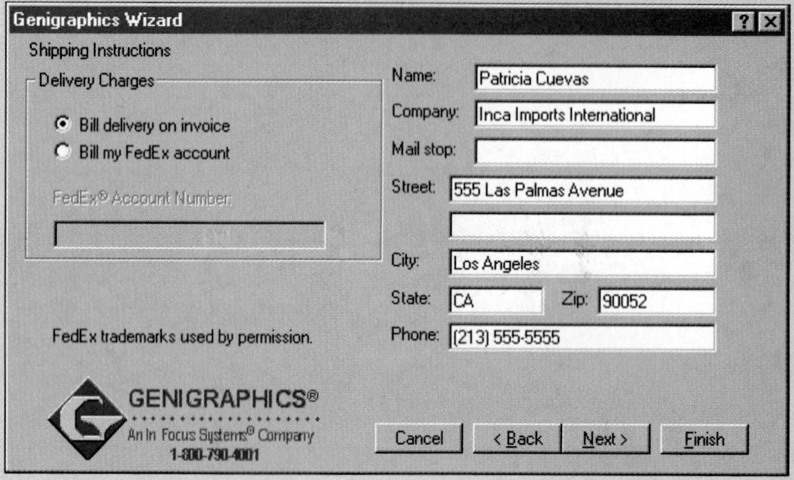

7. Click the **Next** button to display the dialog box for billing information. Make sure **MasterCard** is selected as the method of payment, then enter the fictitious card number **5416-1111-1111-1111**, and then, if necessary, fill out the information about Patricia Cuevas that appears in Figure 4-29.

8. Click the **Next** button to view the last dialog box of the Genigraphics Wizard. Look over the information on the dialog box, and if everything looks correct, click the **Finish** button. The Save As dialog box opens.

TROUBLE? If the last dialog box contains incorrect information, click the Back button to go backward through the Wizard to correct any erroneous information.

Your only task now is to specify that you want to save the Genigraphics file to your Student Disk.

9. In the Save As dialog box, specify the **Tutorial.04** folder, keep the default name Annual Report (Genigraphics will automatically add the filename extension ".gna"), and then click the Save button.

You have now prepared the file Annual Report.gna to send to Genigraphics. If you sent the file to a Genigraphics facility they would create 35mm slides of the presentation.

Preparing Overheads

Patricia's presentation to the stockholders is very important, so she decides to be safe and have you create black-and-white overheads of the presentation in case the slide projector doesn't work. With PowerPoint, you can prepare overhead transparency masters quickly and easily. You simply have to change the slide design to overheads. However, some designs that work well for slides do not work as well for black-and-white overheads, so you should choose a design template that meets your needs. Patricia decides to change the slide design to one that is more appropriate for black-and-white overheads.

To change the presentation design to black-and-white overheads:

1. Click **File**, then click **Slide Setup** to open the Slide Setup dialog box.

2. Click the **Slides Sized for** list arrow and select **Overhead**.

   Patricia wants to change the orientation of the printing from **landscape**, which is wider than it is tall, to **portrait**, which is taller than it is wide. Overheads fit the projector better if they are in portrait orientation.

3. Click the **Portrait** button in the Slides Orientation box, click the **OK** button, and then go to Slide Sorter View. The slides are displayed in portrait orientation. See Figure 4-30.

Figure 4-30
Slides sized for overheads

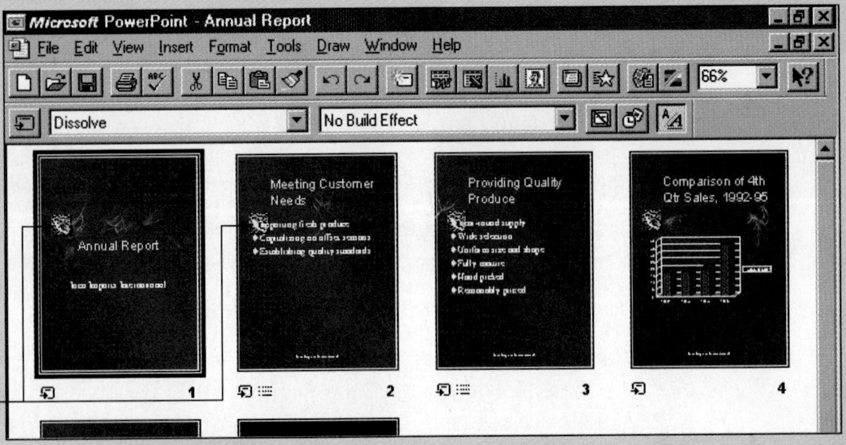

logos in wrong position

As you can see in Figure 4-30, the company logos are now in the wrong position on the slides. On the title slide, Patricia wants you to move the logo below the subtitle, and on the other slides, she wants you to move the logo to the left of the title. To modify the title slide, you will use the **Title Master**, which is similar to the Slide Master, except the Title Master affects only the title slide, not the others. Let's first modify the Title Master, then the Slide Master.

To change the position of the picture on the title slide:

1. Press the **Shift** key and click the **Slide View** button ▣ to display the Slide Master.

2. Click the **New Title Master** button on the status bar. The Title Master appears on the screen.

3. Drag the logo to position it beneath the subtitle. See Figure 4-31.

Figure 4-31 ◀
Title Master

repositioned picture ──────

slide indicator ──────

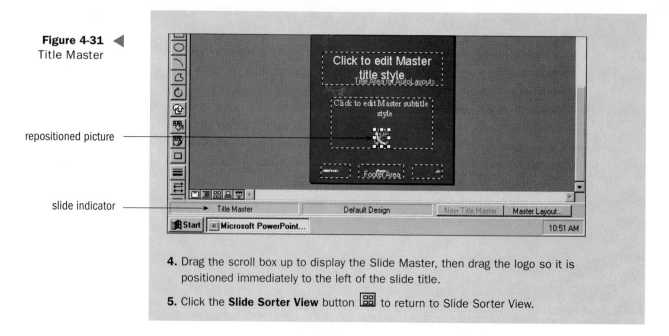

4. Drag the scroll box up to display the Slide Master, then drag the logo so it is positioned immediately to the left of the slide title.

5. Click the **Slide Sorter View** button 🔲 to return to Slide Sorter View.

Your final tasks are to view the slides in black and white (to make sure the current design would make good overhead masters), save the file, and then print the presentation.

To view, save, and print the presentation:

1. Click the **B&W View** button 🔲. The slides are all attractive and legible.

Now Patricia wants you to save the overhead presentation using a different filename.

2. Click **File**, click **Save As**, and then save the presentation to your Student Disk using the filename Annual Report Overheads.

3. Click **File** then click **Print** to open the Print dialog box.

4. Make sure that **Slides (without builds)** is selected in the Print what box and that the **Black & White** option, the **Scale to Fit Paper** option, and the **Frame Slides** options are selected. The Frame Slides option draws a border around each page.

5. Click the **OK** button to print the overhead presentation. This completes the preparation of the presentation.

6. Save your changes and then, if you desire, exit PowerPoint.

Patricia is pleased with the appearance of her overhead masters. She asks her secretary to photocopy the overhead masters onto transparent sheets. Within a few days, Patricia receives her 35mm slides from Genigraphics Corporation. She is ready to give her presentation at the stockholders meeting.

GIVING EFFECTIVE SLIDE SHOW PRESENTATIONS

- Dress appropriately for the meeting.
- Maintain a professional demeanor at all times.
- Introduce yourself and briefly explain what you'll be showing your audience.
- Look at your audience. Make adequate eye contact.
- Speak clearly and audibly.
- If you're using a microphone, adjust it to your height so you won't have to lean down or stretch up to speak into it.
- Keep your language appropriate for the audience and situation. Avoid jargon and slang.
- Summarize your presentation, come to a logical conclusion, and field questions courteously.

Quick Check

1. What is the PowerPoint Viewer? When would you use it?

2. What is the Pack and Go feature?

3. In one sentence, describe how to get 35mm slides made from a PowerPoint slide presentation.

4. Describe what you would do to create overhead masters from your PowerPoint slide presentation.

5. What is the difference between the Slide Master and the Title Master?

Tutorial Assignments

In the following Tutorial Assignment, make sure you click the Blank Presentation button when you start PowerPoint or, if PowerPoint is already running, click the New button on the Standard toolbar to create a new presentation. After working with a presentation and saving your changes, close the presentation.

Do the following:

1. Create a new blank presentation.
2. Create a title slide with the title "Employee Benefits" and the subtitle "Inca Imports International."

3. Using the Slide Master, change the color scheme to give a background color of dark green and a text and line color of solid blue. *Hint*: From the Color Scheme dialog box, click the Custom tab and change the Background and the Text & Lines tiles to the appropriate colors.
4. Change the shade style to From Corner, and the variant with the lightest color in the lower-left corner and the darkest in the upper-right corner.
5. Change the Master title style to a white Arial font.
6. In the Master main text, change the bullet color to light green, but don't change the bullet character.

7. In the second-level text, change the text from blue to gray and the bullet from a dash to a red plus (+). *Hint*: From the Bullet dialog box, you can change the bullet to almost any color by clicking the down arrow under Special Color, then clicking Other Color to display the Other Color dialog box.
8. Insert the Inca logo (from your Student Disk) into the Slide Master. Resize it to the approximate height of the Master title style text box. Position the logo in the lower-right corner of the text box of the Slide Master slide text style, near the text "Object Area for AutoLayouts".

9. Return to Slide View and remove the Inca logo from the title slide. *Hint*: Use the Omit Background Graphic command.

10. Add a new slide with the Bulleted List AutoLayout.

11. Make the title of the new slide "Basic Benefits". Type the following first-level bulleted list items: "Medical and Dental Insurance", "Group Term Life Insurance", "Disability Insurance", "Occupational Accidental Death & Dismemberment Insurance", and "Master Retirement Plan".

12. Insert the existing presentation file "Benefits" from the TAssign folder on your Student Disk into the current presentation.

13. In slide 3, demote the second and third bulleted items because they are the two types of supplemental insurance plans available to Inca Import employees.

14. In slide 6, remove the bullets that appear to the left of the address of the benefits office. *Hint*: Display the Bullets menu, then deselect the checkbox labeled "Use a Bullet".

15. To all the slides, add the transition effect called "Random Bars Vertical".

16. To slides 2 through 5, add the build effect called "Blinds Horizontal". Select the Dim Previous Points option with gray as the dimmed color.

17. Run the slide show to ensure that the builds and transitions work properly.

18. Save the presentation as Supplemental Benefits, then print the presentation in black and white as handouts with six slides per page. Close the file.
    Do the following:

19. Start a new blank presentation, and on the title slide, type the title "Employee of the Month," and the subtitle "Inca Imports International."

20. Using the Slide Master, change the color scheme to a background color of red and a text and lines color of dark blue.

21. Select the background shade style Diagonal Up, and the variant with the lightest color in the upper-left corner and the darkest in the lower-right corner.

22. Change the Master title to white with the 44-point Book Antiqua font. If your computer doesn't have that font, use a different one.

23. Change the Master text styles so the font is 36-point Arial.

24. Draw a large, red star in the middle of the Slide Master to serve as a backdrop for the slides in the presentation. *Hint*: Click the AutoShapes button in the Drawing toolbar, click the Star in the AutoShapes palette, press and hold down the Shift key while you drag from the upper left to the lower right of the slide. (Holding the Shift key maintains the proportions of the image.) Center the star on the slide. Change the star color to solid red by clicking Format, clicking Colors and Lines, then choosing red as the fill color and No Line as the line color. Put the star behind the text by clicking Draw, then clicking Send to Back.

25. Create a footer centered at the bottom of every slide except the title slide with the text "Employee of the Month".

26. Add a new slide with the Title Slide AutoLayout.

27. Make the title of the new slide "Alicia Cardon" and the subtitle "January".

28. Insert the existing presentation file Calendar from the TAssign folder on your Student Disk into the current presentation.

29. To all the slides, add a transition effect and an automatic advance time, using the following method: In Slide Sorter View, select all the slides, then click the Slide Transition button on the Formatting toolbar to display the Slide Transition dialog box. Change the Effect to "Cover Right". Set the speed to "Slow". In the Advance box, click Automatically after, then set the time to four seconds.

30. Set the slide show to run continuously. *Hint*: Click View, click Slide Show, click Use Slide Timings, and click Loop Continuously Until "Esc".

31. Start the slide show and watch as the presentation automatically moves from one slide to the next and returns to the first slide after showing the last slide. If the slide show isn't automatic and continuous, you have made a mistake in one of the previous steps. Review the steps and fix your mistake.

32. Press the Esc key to end the slide show after you've watched the entire presentation at least once.

33. Save the presentation as Employee Calendar and then print the first three slides of the presentation in black and white. Close the file.

Case Problems

1. Training on Sexual Harassment Katherine Jaidar is the Director of Human Resources Development for McNeil Manufacturing Company, a large manufacturer of gardening supplies—rakes, hoes, shovels, hoses, sprinkling systems, and tillers. One of her responsibilities is to provide training to McNeil employees on sexual harassment in the workplace. She prepares a PowerPoint slide presentation for her training classes that will double as a self-training presentation. Do the following:

1. Create a blank presentation with a title slide. Make the title "Sexual Harassment in the Workplace", the first line of the subtitle, "Training for employees of", and the second line of the subtitle "McNeil Manufacturing Company".

2. From the Slide Master, change the color scheme to give a background color of light blue and a text and lines color of black.

3. Change the background shade style to Vertical, and choose the variant with the darkest color on the left and lightest color on the right.

4. Change the Master title style to the 40-point Arial font.

5. In the Master text style line (the first level in the bulleted list), change the bullet color to yellow, but don't change the bullet style.

6. Return to Slide View, and add a new slide with the Bulleted List AutoLayout. Make the title "Definition of Sexual Harassment", and type the following bulleted items: "Promise of career advancement for sexual favors", "Threats of career jeopardy if sexual demands are rejected", and "Deliberate, repeated, unsolicited comments, gestures, or physical actions of a sexual nature".

7. Insert the file Harass from the Cases folder on your Student Disk after slide 2 of the current presentation.

8. On the new slide 3, reduce the size of the text box of the main text, and move the box down on the slide, so the slide appears more balanced top to bottom.

9. To the two slides with the titles "Don'ts" and "Do's," add an appropriate clip-art image. Resize the text boxes on the screen so they will fit on the slide, if necessary.

10. Add "Fly from Bottom" build effects to all the slides that have bulleted lists. Include the feature to dim previous points using an appropriate color of your own choice.

11. To all the slides, add the transition effect called "Checkerboard Across" with a slow speed. *Hint:* You can set the transition speed on the Transition dialog box.

12. Check the spelling in your presentation. *Hint:* Begin by clicking Tools, then click Spelling.

13. Run the slide show to ensure that the builds and transitions work properly, save the presentation as **Case 1 - Harassment Policy**, then print all the slides of the presentation in black and white.

14. Close the file.

2. Report on Using a Presentation Graphics Program You have agreed to give a presentation to a college fraternity on the benefits of using a presentation graphics program like PowerPoint. As you prepare your presentation using PowerPoint, use proper principles of planning and design as discussed throughout this book. Specifically, do the following:

1. Create a blank presentation with a title slide. Choose your own title, but use your name as the subtitle.

2. From the Slide Master, change the background color to blue, change the shade style to Horizontal, and choose the variant with the darkest color at the top and lightest color at the bottom.

3. Change the Master title style to Arial font and the color to yellow, and change all the text in the Master text styles to the color white.

4. In the Master text style line (the first level in the bulleted list), change the bullet color to yellow, but don't change the bullet character.

5. In the Slide Master, insert an appropriate clip-art image (such as a computer or a diskette). Make sure the clip-art image is simple enough so it can be seen clearly when reduced to a smaller size. Reduce the size so that the image is not more than about an inch in any dimension. Position the image in the lower-right corner of the text box of the Slide Master text style, near the text "Object Area for AutoLayouts."

6. Add the same graphic to the Title Master as you did to the Slide Master, only make it smaller and position it below the subtitle.

7. Add at least four new slides with the Bulleted List AutoLayout. For example, you might create a slide with the title "Advantages of Presentation Programs" and a list of advantages such as "Easy to use," "Easy to modify," "Professional quality," "Flexible," and so forth. Another example might be a title such as "Weaknesses of Presentation Programs" and a list of disadvantages such as "Requires expensive hardware," "Difficult to get appropriate clip art," and so forth. Other possible titles include "Key Features of Presentation Software," "Possible Uses of Presentation Software," and "Steps in Learning How to Use Presentation Software."

8. Add a slide with a graph so your audience can see a sample graph or chart. For example, the title might be "Cost of Presentation Software," with a bar graph for the cost of PowerPoint, Harvard Graphics, Novell Presentations, and Adobe Persuasion. If you can't easily obtain real numbers, make up some reasonable prices.

9. Add a summary slide with a bulleted list of the most important ideas in your presentation.

10. Add "Dissolve" build effects to all of the slides that have bulleted lists. Include the feature to dim previous points.

11. To all the slides, add the transition effect called "Uncover Right-Down" with a slow speed. *Hint*: You can set the transition speed in the Transition dialog box.

12. Create speaker's notes for all of your slides. Include whatever information you need to help you with your presentation. *Hint*: In Notes Pages View, zoom the page to 100% to type your notes.

13. Check the spelling in your presentation. *Hint*: Begin by clicking Tools, then clicking Spelling.

14. Run the slide show to ensure that the builds and transitions work properly.

15. Save the presentation as Case 2 - Presentation Programs, print all the slides of the presentation, and then print the speaker's notes in black and white.

16. Create the file Case 2 - Presentation Programs.gna that could be sent to Genigraphics for preparation of 35mm slides.

17. Using the techniques you learned in this tutorial, modify the presentation for creating black-and-white overhead transparencies.

18. Save the overhead version of the presentation as Case 2 - Presentation Overheads, then print the overhead masters.

19. Close the file.

3. Presentation on Personal Interests Create a presentation on one of your personal interests, hobbies, or college courses. Your presentation might be on such topics as playing the piano, learning Spanish, astronomy, computer games, movies, horseback riding, physical fitness, or cooking—anything that you're interested in and have some knowledge about. Do the following:

1. Choose an appropriate and attractive color scheme, background shading, and fonts.

2. Create a presentation of at least seven slides, including a title slide, at least three slides with bulleted lists, at least one slide with a graph or chart, a summary slide, and a blank slide (one with a black background) to signal the end of the presentation.
3. Add clip art to the Slide Master.

4. Include speaker's notes on all the slides. *Hint*: In Notes Pages View, zoom the page to 100% to type your notes.
5. Check the spelling of your presentation by clicking Tools, then clicking Spelling, and following the instructions on the Spelling dialog box.
6. Add transition effects for all slides. Add build effects (with dimming of previous points) for all slides with bulleted lists.
7. Save the presentation as Case 3 - My Hobby on your Student Disk, then print the slides as handouts (with three or six slides per page), and print the speaker's notes in black and white.
8. Prepare the file Case 3 - My Hobby.gna for commercial preparation of 35mm slides by Genigraphics Corporation.
9. Close the file.

4. Presentation on Using PowerPoint in the Classroom Now that you understand how to use PowerPoint, you know what a powerful program it is, and how it can enhance classroom lectures at your school. Prepare a presentation that includes information about the features of PowerPoint that you have learned, and a description of each. Prepare the presentation as if you were giving it to a group of professors at your school who aren't aware of the advantages of using PowerPoint in the classroom. Create a new presentation with an appropriate template. Include at least eight slides in the presentation. Structure your presentation so it includes information about the capabilities of PowerPoint and provide examples of each. For example, you might include slides on using clip art, graphs and charts, or transition and build effects on slides. You might also want to discuss the advantages of using PowerPoint to create a Viewer disk, 35mm slides, or black-and-white overhead transparencies. Make sure that your presentation discusses the features of PowerPoint and persuades a positive audience to use the program in the classroom, When you are done with your slides, view the slide show, print handouts (as two slides per page) of the presentation, save the presentation using the filename Case 4-PowerPoint Presentation, and then close the file.

Answers to Quick Check Questions

SESSION 1.1

1 PowerPoint allows you to produce effective presentations in the form of black-and-white or color overheads, 35-mm photographic slides, or on-screen slides. Using PowerPoint, you can prepare each component of your presentation: individual slides, speaker's notes, an outline of your presentation, and audience handouts. PowerPoint also allows you to create a consistent format for each of these components and to manipulate text and add graphics to your presentations.

2 a. A PowerPoint presentation is a file that contains slides and possibly speaker's notes, handouts, and an outline.
   b. The slide master is a slide that contains the text and graphics that will appear on every slide of a particular kind in the presentation.
   c. A template is a predefined format and color scheme for your presentation.

3 What is my purpose or objective for this presentation? What type of presentation is needed? Who is the audience? What information does that audience need? What is the physical location of my presentation? What is the best format for presenting the information contained in this presentation, given the location of the presentation?

4 Click the PowerPoint icon on the Microsoft Office shortcut bar, or click the Start button, move the mouse pointer to Programs, and then move the mouse pointer to Microsoft PowerPoint.

5 When you start PowerPoint, click the Open an Existing Presentation button in the PowerPoint startup dialog box (or click File then click Open).

6 Click File, click Save As, select the location (drive and folder) in which you want to save the file, type the new filename in the File name box, and click the OK button.

7 a. The status bar tells you which slide you're working on, the design template for the current presentation, and, when you move the mouse pointer to a command button, provides a description of the command. The status bar also contains shortcut buttons: the New Slide button and the Slide Layout button.
   b. The ToolTip is a yellow square containing the name of the button on which the mouse pointer is resting.
   c. The Standard toolbar allows you to select many of the standard Windows and PowerPoint commands, such as opening an existing presentation, saving your current presentation to disk, printing the presentation, and cutting and pasting text and graphics.
   d. The Formatting toolbar allows you to format the text of your presentations.
   e. The View toolbar contains buttons that allow you to change the way you view a slide presentation.
   f. A build slide is a slide on which the bulleted text progressively appears on the screen, one item at a time, during a slide presentation.

8 a. Slide View allows you to see and edit text and graphics on an individual slide.
   b. Slide Sorter View allows you to view miniature images of all the slides at once, change the order of the slides, or set special features for your slide show.
   c. Slide Show View allows you to view (or show) the presentation in full-screen view, that is, just as it will appear when you make your presentation.

9 To advance: press the spacebar or click the left mouse button. To go back: press the Backspace key or click the right mouse button.

SESSION 1.2

1 a. Outline View allows you to view the outline of your presentation and to edit your presentation in text mode.
   b. Notes Pages View allows you view and edit your presentation notes on individual slides.

2 To see how your slides will look when you print them on a black-and-white (noncolor) printer.

3 Click File, click Print, then in the Print what box, select Note Pages.

4 Click Help on the menu bar, click Microsoft PowerPoint Help Topics, type "clip," select a topic on clip art that you want to view, and then click the Display button.

5 Use the Help button on the Standard toolbar.

6 a. From the help topic "Using Design Templates to give your presentation a consistent look": Design Templates contain color schemes, slide and title masters with custom formatting, and styled fonts that have been designed for a particular "look." When you apply a Design Template to your presentation, the slide master and color scheme of the new template replace the slide master and color scheme of the presentation.
   b. The Format Painter allows you to copy the format (color scheme, design) of one slide onto another slide.
   c. "A transition is the special effect you use to introduce a slide during a slide show. For example, you can fade in from black or dissolve from one slide to another."

SESSION 2.1

1 The AutoContent Wizard helps you create an outline based on the category and length of your presentation.

2 A disadvantage of the AutoContent Wizard is that it provides sample text. If you don't want that text, you have to delete it and type your own. Another disadvantage is that your presentation might not fit into one of the pre-defined categories.

3 a. A placeholder is a region of a slide reserved for inserting text or graphics.
   b. To select something means to make it active usually by highlighting or marking it. You select something by clicking it or by dragging the pointer over it. You can then delete or modify the selected item.
   c. The title on a slide is the text that is usually large and at the top of a slide that states the purpose or topic of the slide
   d. The main text of a slide is the bulleted list.

4 a. Select the text, then press the Backspace key or the Delete key.
   b. Click the Outline button on the View bar to switch to Outline view; click the Slide View button to switch to Slide view.

5 To display only the slide titles in Outline view, click the Show Titles button on the Outlining toolbar.

6 Use six or fewer items per screen, and use incomplete sentences of six or fewer words.

7 Select a placeholder by clicking the icon to its left or by dragging the pointer over the text.

SESSION 2.2

1 a. Select the text of an outline item, then click the Move Up button on the Outline toolbar. Or, select the text, then drag it up to the new location.
   b. Click the slide icon to the left of the slide title, then press the Backspace key or the Delete key, or click Edit, then click Delete Slide.
   c. Select the text and type the new text.
   d. Drag the I-beam pointer icon to select the text and then delete or retype it.

2 Promote means to unindent or increase the level of an outline item.

3 Demote means to indent or decrease the level of an outline item.

4 The benefit of Outline view over Slide view is that in Outline view you can see the text of several slides at once, where it's easier to work with text. The benefit of Slide view is that you can see the design and layout of the slide.

SESSION 2.3

1 a. Select the text, then click the Text Color button on the Formatting toolbar.
   b. Select the text, then click the Increase Font Size button on the Formatting toolbar.
   c. Move the insertion point to the end of the text of the slide prior to the one you want to create, press Enter, and (if necessary) click the Promote button one or more times to promote to a title level.
   d. Select the text, click the Cut button, move the insertion point to a new location, then click the Paste button.
   e. Select the text, put the pointer in the selected area, press the left mouse button and drag the selected text to the new location, and release the mouse button.

2 A design template is file that specifies the colors and format of the background and the type style of the titles, accents, and text in a presentation.

3 a. A font is a set of characters (letters, digits, and other characters such as !, @, and *) that have a certain design and appearance.
   b. Points are a measure of the height of a font. One point is $\frac{1}{72}$ of an inch.
   c. A serif font is one that has little embellishments at the ends of the line strokes on each character.
   d. A sans serif font is a font that lacks serifs.

4 Click the Undo button on the Standard toolbar.

5 The advantage of cut and paste over drag and drop is that it is easier to make long-distance moves, for example, to other slides. Also, after cutting, you can paste in as many copies of the cut text as you want. The advantage of drag and drop is that it is easier to move text a short distance, for example, on the same line.

6 Click the Apply Design Template button on the Standard toolbar, select the design template filename, and click the Apply button.

SESSION 3.1

1 a. Click anywhere within the text, then click the edge of the text box.
   b. Select the text box so that the resize handles appear, then drag a resize handle to the new location.
   c. Select the text box so that the resize handles appear, then drag the edge of the text box.
   d. Select the text box, then click the Left Alignment button on the Formatting toolbar.

2 a. Click Insert, then click Picture. Select the picture file from a disk, then click the OK button.
   b. From Slide View, with the desired slide in the presentation window, click the Slide Layout button on the status bar.
   c. Click the Insert Clip Art button on the Standard toolbar, select the desired clip-art image from the Microsoft ClipArt Gallery, then click the Insert button.
   d. Click Format, click Custom Background, click the check box "Omit Background Graphics from Master," and then click the Apply button.

3 Situations to use graphics effectively: to present information that words can't communicate effectively; to interest and motivate the reader; to communicate relationships quickly; to increase understanding and retention.

4 To remove or move one of several objects within the clip-art image.

5 a. Slide Layout: a predefined arrangement of placeholders on the slide for inserting the slide title, text, or graphics.
   b. clip art: an image from the Microsoft ClipArt Gallery.
   c. object: any item (text box, clip art, graph, organization chart, picture) on a slide that you can move, resize, rotate, or otherwise manipulate.
   d. resize handles: small squares in the corners and on the edges of a text or graphics box that, when dragged with the pointer, change the size of the box.

6 Selecting an appropriate type of graphic: consider your audience: job, experience, education, culture; consider your purpose: to inform, persuade, instruct, identify, interest, motivate; consider the type of information on the slide: numerical values, logical relationships, procedures and processes, visual and spatial characteristics.

SESSION 3.2

1 Change the Slide Layout to Text & Graph or Graph & Text, double-click the graph placeholder, edit the information in the datasheet, click anywhere outside the datasheet, then click anywhere outside the graph box.

2 Change the Slide Layout of the desired slide to Organization Chart; double-click the organization chart placeholder; type the personnel names, positions, and other information into the boxes of the organization chart; add subordinate and co-worker boxes as desired; click File, click Exit and Return to (presentation name), then click the Yes button.

3 a. Subordinate is a box that goes beneath another box in the organization chart.
   b. Co-worker is a box that goes on the left or the right side of another box in an organizational chart.

4 A diagram of boxes, connected with lines, showing the hierarchy of positions within an organization.

5 A grid of cells, similar to a Microsoft Excel spreadsheet, in which you can add data and labels.

6 Press the Tab key or Enter, or click the pointer in the cell.

SESSION 3.3

1 Click the appropriate tool on the Draw toolbar, move the pointer into the slide area, and drag the pointer to draw the object.

2 A tool that allows you to draw predefined shapes, such as triangles and squares.

3 With the object selected, click Format, click Colors and Lines, select the desired fill color, then click the OK button.

4 With the triangle selected, click Draw, click Rotate/Flip, then click Flip Vertical.

5 With the object selected, click the Free Rotate button on the Draw toolbar, then drag one of the corner resize handles of the object.

SESSION 4.1

1 Major items to prepare for a presentation meeting: (1) prepare an agenda; (2) prepare the presentation; (3) check the physical arrangements; (4) check the equipment; (5) prepare other items as needed.

2 a. the shading of the background color, for example, dark at the top and gradually going lighter toward the bottom
   b. one of the variations of a particular background color, for example, one variant might be light in the lower-left corner and dark in the upper-left corner, while another variant might be dark in the lower-left corner and light in the upper-right corner.

3 The Slide Master is a slide that contains text and graphics that appear on all the slides (except the title slide) in the presentation and controls the format and color of the text and background on all slides. You would use the Slide Master any time you want to add a graphic or text to all the slides in the presentation.

4 Starting with a blank slide presentation allows you to add text and slides without having to delete the placeholders of the AutoContent Wizard.

5 a. Press the Shift key, then click the Slide View button; or click View, click Master, then click Slide Master.
   b. Click Format, click Slide Color Scheme, click the Standard tab, click the desired background, and click the Apply or Apply to All button.
   c. Click Format, click Custom Background, click the Down arrow next to the Background Fill, click Shaded, click the desired shade style and variant, click the OK button, then click the Apply or Apply to All button.
   d. If desired, display the Slide Master, click anywhere within the text of the bulleted item, click Format, click Bullet, change to the desired style, select a font using the Bullets From list, then click the desired character, click the Special Color palette checkbox, click the desired color tile, then click the OK button.

6 In Slide Master View, click Insert, then click Picture, change the drive and folder and select the filename, then click the OK button. Resize and move the picture as necessary.

SESSION 4.2

1   a. text near the bottom of a slide that contains information such as the date and time, slide number, company name, or the title of the presentation.
    b. a method of moving one slide off the screen and bringing another slide onto the screen during a slide show
    c. a feature that allows you to progressively display individual bulleted items, one item at a time.
    d. to mark a slide with the pointer pen during a slide presentation.

2   a. Click Insert, click Slides from File, select the presentation file, click the Insert button.
    b. In Slide Sorter View, select the slide or slides, click the down arrow button in the Transition Effects box, and click the desired effect.
    c. In Slide Sorter View, select the slide or slides, click the down arrow button in the Build Effects box, click the desired build effect.

3   You would add a footer if you wanted the same information at the bottom of each slide. To add a footer, click View, click Header and Footer, click the Footer checkbox, type the text of the footer, click the Apply to All button.

4   Advantage: add interest to the slide show. Disadvantage: can distract your audience from your message.

5   Advantage: focuses audiences attention on the current item you're discussing. Disadvantage: dimmed bulleted items may be hard to read and refer to later on.

6   Press the left arrow key.

SESSION 4.3

1   A separate program that you can use to show a presentation on any Windows 95 or Windows NT computer. You would use it to show a presentation on a computer that doesn't have PowerPoint installed.

2   A feature that allows you to create a Viewer disk that contains the PowerPoint Viewer files and a copy of the presentation.

3   Use the Genigraphics Wizard to create a special file that you can send to Genigraphics to order slides from a presentation.

4   Change the slide setup to Overhead and to Portrait, then print the presentation.

5   Slide Master allows you to change the format of, or add text or graphics to, all the slides except the title slide. Title Master allows you to change the format of, or add text or graphics to, the title slide of your presentation

Microsoft PowerPoint 7 **Task Reference**

TASK	PAGE #	RECOMMENDED METHOD
35mm Slides, format slides for	PP 108	Click File, click Slide Setup, select Slides Sized for 35mm Slides, click the OK button
35mm Slides, prepare to send to Genigraphics	PP 108	Format the slides for 35mm slides, click File, click Send to Genigraphics, follow Genigraphics Wizard
Background color, change	PP 90	Click Format, click Custom Background, select the desired background color and shading, click the Apply or Apply to All button
Background graphic, remove Master, click	PP 60	Click Format, click Custom Background, click Omit Background Graphics from the Master, then click the Apply button
Black & White, view	PP 18	Click
Build effects, dim previous items	PP 102	Click Tools, click Build Slide Text, click Other; click on the After Build Step list arrow, click the tile of the desired color, then click the OK button
Bullets, remove	PP 33	Click anywhere in the text of the bulleted item, click Format, click Bullet, click Use a Bullet checkbox to delete, click the OK button
Color Scheme, change	PP 88	Click Format, click Slide Color Scheme, click the desired color scheme, click the Apply or Apply to All button
Design Template, change	PP 44	Click , click the name of the desired template file, click the Apply button
First slide, go to		Press Ctrl+Home
Footer, insert	PP 98	Click View, click Header and Footer, click the Footer checkmark, type the footer text, click the Apply or Apply to All button
Graph, insert	PP 67	Click the Slide Layout button, click a Graph layout, click the Apply button, double-click the graph box placeholder, create the graph
Header, insert		Click View, click Header and Footer, click the Header checkmark, type the header text, click the Apply or Apply to All button
Last slide, go to		Press Ctrl+End
Next slide, go to	PP 14	In Slide View, click
Notes Pages View	PP 17	Click
Object, flip	PP 76	Select the object, click Draw, click Rotate/Flip, click Flip Vertical or Flip Horizontal
Object, rotate	PP 78	Select the object, click , drag a resize handle
Objects, align	PP 59	Shift-click to select objects, click Draw, click Align, click alignment position
Objects, group		Select the objects, click Draw, click Group
Objects, ungroup	PP 67	Select the object, click Draw, click Ungroup
Outline text, demote (indent more)	PP 36	Place insertion point in paragraph, click or press Tab

Microsoft PowerPoint 7 **Task Reference**

TASK	PAGE #	RECOMMENDED METHOD
Outline text, move	PP 36	Click slide icon, or click bullet, click ⬆ or ⬇
Outline text, promote (indent less)	PP 36	Place insertion point in paragraph, click ⬅ or press Shift+Tab
Outline View	PP 11	Click 🗒
Overheads, prepare	PP 110	Click File, click Slide Setup, select Slides Sized for Overhead, click the desired orientation (usually Portrait), click the OK button
Pack and Go Wizard	PP 106	Click File, click Pack And Go, continue through Wizard
Previous slide, go to		In Slide View, click ⬆
Properties, file, display	PP 94	Click File, click Properties
Shape, create	PP 75	Click 🔲, click desired shape, drag pointer to draw and size the shape
Slide Master, view	PP 89	Shift-click 🔲
Slide Show, exit		Press the Esc key, or right click mouse and select end show
Slide Show, view		Click 🖵; press Spacebar or click left mouse button to advance; press Backspace or press right mouse button to go back
Slide Sorter View	PP 12	Click 🔳
Slide View	PP 11	Click 🔲
Slide, annotate during Slide Show	PP 104	Click ✎ or right click mouse, click Pen, make annotation
Slide, delete	PP 38	In Slide View, click Edit, click Delete Slide
Slide, new, insert	PP 42	Click 🔲
Slides from another presentation, insert	PP 96	Click Insert, click Slides from File, select the disk and folder, click the filename, click the Insert button
Spelling, check		Click ✓
Text box, create	PP 77	Click 🅰, click pointer on the slide, type the text
Text, align	PP 59	Select text box, click Format, click Alignment, click the desired alignment (Left, Right, Center, Justify)
View, Slide Sorter	PP 12	Click 🔳
Viewer, start	PP 106	Place disk with "Pack and Go" file into drive A, click Start button on Windows 95 taskbar, click Run, type "a:pngsetup", click the OK button, type folder for viewer, click the OK button, click Yes
Zoom	PP 17	Click View, click Zoom, click the desired zoom value, click the OK button

Microsoft PowerPoint 7 for Windows 95 Brief **Index**